Finding True Love *after* Heartbreak *and* Disappointment

Finding True Love *after* Heartbreak *and* Disappointment

A New THING

LYDIA LUCAS

VINE
PUBLISHING

Unless otherwise indicated, Scriptures are taken from the Holy Bible, New International Version®, NIV® Copyright © 1973, 1978, 1984, 2011 by Biblica, Inc.™ Used by permission. All rights reserved worldwide.

Scripture quotations marked (NLT) are taken from the Holy Bible, New Living Translation, copyright ©1996, 2004, 2015 by Tyndale House Foundation. Used by permission of Tyndale House Publishers, a Division of Tyndale House Ministries, Carol Stream, Illinois 60188. All rights reserved.

Scripture quotations marked MSG are from The Message. Copyright © Eugene H. Peterson 1993, 1994, 1995, 1996, 2000, 2001, 2002 by Tyndale House Foundation. Used by permission of Tyndale House Publishers, Inc., Carol Stream, Illinois 60188. All rights reserved.

Vine Publishing's name and logo are trademarks of Vine Publishing, Inc.

ISBN: 978-0-9856535-9-0 (paperback)
ISBN: 978-0-578-78530-1 (e-book)

Library of Congress Cataloging-in-Publication Data
Library of Congress Control Number: 2020920226

Published by Vine Publishing, Inc.
New York, NY
www.vinepublish.com

Printed in the United States of America

Thank you, mom and dad, for your unrelenting prayers and support. Mom, you never stopped hoping. I love you. Thank you to my honey for loving me, talking me through the moments of ridiculous doubt and for endless hours of watching the kids so I could escape to write. Thank you to the prayer warriors that I have the honor of calling friends. Thank you to every person in these pages who has left an impact on my life. Thank you to Taneki for believing in what this book could be. Thank you Denya for the encouragement.

Most importantly, my dear sweet Lord, this book and my life are nothing without you. I love you so much. May this book bring you glory.

TABLE *of* CONTENTS

INTRODUCTION

I sat in the back of my father's two-door Pontiac on a bright Sunday morning in early June, trying really hard not to throw up. My mom was in the front passenger seat, and even though she did not say a word to me, in my mind, I could hear her sarcastically letting me have it in her Nuyorican accent: "That's why we drink, right?"

In my mind, she said it in Spanish, which automatically doubles the intensity. Every time I felt the surge of saliva collecting in my mouth, that telltale sign that the contents of my stomach would soon come back up, I swallowed and tried to take a deep breath so my parents would not notice how bad off I really was. My daughter, plump and cheerful at almost two years old, sat in her car seat next to me, blissfully unaware of my misery. My father's car intermittently had air conditioning, and I cannot now remember if this was one of those times when it was actually working. The drive to the West Side across Central Park on 97th street could feel excruciatingly long and cruelly twisty if you are hungover like I was on that early summer morning back in 2000. I had just graduated college and celebrated my birthday by going on a night cruise around the city with some of my sorority sisters. To celebrate me, many friends bought me drinks, none of which I refused. I also did not seem to care that I was mixing both dark and light liquors, a sure-fire way to ensure one's demise. Hence, here I was, on a Sunday morning, in the back of my father's old sedan that probably had no air conditioning, trying to hold back the urge to puke all over the place, and wishing I could have just stayed in bed.

I wasn't still in bed because my mother—partly as a punishment tactic, I suspect—made me get up to go with them to the church she had been attending over the last year. I am the oldest of three kids, and while neither my brother nor sister, both of whom also still lived at home, was made to go, she probably felt that I, especially in my present state, a hungover single mother, needed some Jesus in my life. That religious Jesus freak bug I had seen take a couple of people down back at school had bitten my mom really good, and I was a target, not even able to have what I would have considered a proper hangover, sprawled on the bathroom floor and holding on to a toilet seat for dear life. Instead, I had to be on my way to church, of all places. The only thing I wanted from Jesus right then was to make it all go away.

As the car went down Columbus Avenue at what felt like a snail's pace, I felt saliva rising forcefully and realized that no amount of swallowing and deep breaths could help me now.

"I need a bag," I uttered. My mom passed me a plastic bag and my daughter turned and looked at me completely straight-faced, with her dark, almond-shaped baby eyes boring into me. Why did I suddenly feel judged by a toddler? I didn't have time to fully ponder this as I finally lost the ability to keep it together, retched into the bag and felt the initial relief that comes after finally letting it out.

"Can I go home now?" I asked my mother, who I could tell was so through with me.

"Fine, but let this be a lesson to stop drinking like that!" she said in a stern tone. Even then I knew she was holding back on really letting me have it.

"Okay," I sighed in sweet relief as my father dropped her and my daughter off at church on the Upper West Side and made the trip back home to East Harlem where I could finally vomit and sleep it off as I wished.

I am starting this book off here, in this uncomely and awkward place, because I want you to know that I am not one of those seemingly perfect church women who wore a purity ring through her teen and college years and soon after, met the love of her life and lost her virginity on her wedding night. I was and am flawed, and for a long time, I thought God was not for women like me. Women who have lived too hard to be lovable by God or a godly man. I thought I could only fear God and live in shame before Him for choices I had made. The last thing I thought and expected was for God to care for and bless me. I have told the story many times when I speak to women's groups, about how many of those early days in church were a haze as I was either on two or three hours of sleep, or still a bit hung over. I have shared my missteps, desperate choices, flat-out hard-headedness and also how, in spite of all of these factors that should have sent me on a trajectory for complete disaster, God showed His relentlessly-loving self to me. God smiled on me and my life and changed it from the inside out.

I have to tell you this first so that as you read what has taken me a lot of vulnerability to share with you, you will know that I can relate to mess. I can relate to desperation, hopelessness, pride. I can relate to being sick of it all, of wanting to give up, and of wondering "when, God, when?!"

I am not special or a favorite of God (He has no favorites). I am not stronger or smarter or more charming than any of you beautiful women reading this page. All I did was *surrender*. That is one simple word which signifies the hardest thing I have ever done. And it didn't happen overnight either! In this book, which, beyond a shadow of a doubt, has been commissioned by God for His daughters, you will read about my journey as a single mom who was still growing up herself, about my disastrous forays into the world of dating and pseudo love, about me making the same mistakes over and over and over...ALL the mess, girl! But the best part is that in all of those cringe-worthy moments, God also taught me some things that have been life-changing. I've learned about waiting, about being still and trusting God through heart-wrenching moments and about being obedient, even when I looked good and crazy. I can't get over the fact that God didn't throw me away because of my stuff, but He drew me in and used my stuff so I could help someone else in the midst of her own stuff. So, that being said, I invite you to my journey and I pray with every fiber of my being that you are blessed by what I am going to share.

PART ONE

HEARTBREAK

CHAPTER *One*

A BUMPY RIDE

I was hung over on many Sunday mornings. I mean, Sunday morning comes after Saturday night—what did anyone expect? I made sure not to go over the limit to a sloppy vomit state after one instance of throwing up in the back of my father's car, but did have quite a few episodes in the balcony of the church (where I could remain unnoticed) with nausea, headaches and exhaustion from getting little to no sleep. I went to church because my mother forced me——wait, she will probably read this—I mean, *strongly encouraged* me to go and I didn't have it in me to refuse. Well, maybe that's not entirely true. I mean, I could have put my foot down— being twenty-two years old and all—but I wasn't really averse to the whole God thing. God was okay with me, in moderation. After all, this wasn't exactly my first foray into Christianity.

Growing up, my parents were not church-going people. My next-door neighbor, who had kids around our age, would take my brother and me along with her family to the Second Spanish Baptist Church a couple of blocks away. At this church, which was bilingual, we attended Sunday school and I learned about the important basics of who Jesus was, what the cross meant and stories of some of the OG's like Moses and Abraham. We even attended Christian summer camp in Pennsylvania with other kids from the church from ages 9–12. Every year, I looked forward to sleeping in a cabin, canoe rides, the snack shop, crafts like basket weaving and painting pottery, daily swims, a symphony of crickets at night lulling me to sleep and the playing of a trumpet in the morning to cheerfully wake me up. These people sure knew how to do the camp thing right! It was just like the movies I had seen, minus the inappropriate high jinx! As what could only be the best bonus ever, I also experienced God at camp. I memorized Bible verses like John 3:16 and sang songs about being a missionary every day and the Lord being more precious than silver and gold. I was awestruck by my teenage counselors who were the coolest people ever to walk the earth to me and enjoyed our evening devotions led by them. I absolutely loved church camp (as I called it) and accepted the Lord as my Savior every summer, just to be sure it stuck. When my brother and I would come home from camp, we were little evangelists, sharing the good news with our parents with reckless abandon.

Once in the sixth grade, our teacher brought in someone to speak to us about Judaism. I think we had been reading the Diary of Anne Frank, so this was part of the learning unit. Anyhow, the guest told us they knew a special language called Hebrew. My hand shot up in the air and I exclaimed excitedly before even being called on by my teacher.

"I know a song in Hebrew that I learned at camp". I then sang, in the most angelic voice I could muster, a song about Jesus being

Lord, to this Jewish woman who was likely the only other person in the room who understood what I was singing.

Ummm, awkward. My teacher didn't know whether she should be impressed or embarrassed. She was likely a bit of both. I was beaming with pride that my little bit of Hebrew had come in handy. *You're welcome everyone*, I thought. Church camp and Second Spanish Baptist served me well in those elementary years.

Transition came after my last year at Camp Streamside when, at twelve years old, I stopped going to church. Can you guess how the story went from there? Adolescence and an awareness of what was perceived as cool and socially acceptable set in. My fire for the Lord was quenched and replaced with zeal for friends, material things, and boys. My life was like the lives of many other young people around me, and I had many highs and lows that come with growing up. There was fighting at home, often to the point of the police being called, stemming from my father's alcoholism. Still, my siblings and I thrived though and we shared tons of good memories from growing up. We often struggled financially, so I started working from the age of fourteen so I could buy sneakers and designer clothes. I dreamed of making my own life so different from the parts I loathed in my youth. I looked for affirmation, affection and acceptance from friends. If I could achieve what I deemed to be normal, like trendy clothes, boys doting over me, bamboo earrings (at least two pairs), a Fendi bag, and a bad attitude like the LL Cool J song, then I could prove to myself that I was not dysfunctional, regardless of what home looked like sometimes. So, this pursuit of my concept of normalcy and having more than what I grew up with was my focus, and I depended on myself to achieve it. I didn't need God. I would go to heaven when all was said and done, of that I was pretty sure, but the time in-between had nothing to do with Him.

Pursuing my own happiness in my own way continued through high school and beyond college, and many times, the pursuit was to my own detriment. In trying to be "happy", I also made a lot of choices I am not proud of, and I was often downright foolish. Nonetheless, I made it through college, despite the number of times my happiness plan backfired, and even after having a baby in my sophomore year. This achievement was due in large part to my parents.

By 1997, the year I became pregnant, my mom had encountered God for herself after being at wits' end herself. She had joined the local Catholic church, which had become much more charismatic and met her where she was. When I was home one weekend from school and told her that I was pregnant (well, she actually told me—mother's intuition), she said that she was now a follower of Jesus and did not believe in abortion. She said that she would help me in any way she could as long as I finished school and accepted the fact that I likely would be a single mom (she was right). After an emotionally challenging pregnancy and completely breaking away from my boyfriend, I had Kiera in October of that year. I resolved to finish school and finish strong. I lived on campus at Hofstra University and would get my daughter on the weekends where she would be doted upon by friends and sorority sisters. Essentially, my parents raised my daughter for the first two years of her life. In many ways, my daughter's birth brought healing to my family. In the wake of becoming a grandpa, my father made considerable changes in his life, and after being separated from my mom for some time, he went back home. Even my brother, who was a moody recluse of a middle child with body piercings and black nail polish, stayed up late nights rocking Kiera and cuddling her. I had so much support from family and friends that despite having separated from Kiera's father during my pregnancy, there was no shortage of love and provision for this baby girl. I got refocused and once back at school, stayed on the Dean's list until I graduated.

I finished school, had a very vibrant social life, dated, and was on my way to a career and stable life for my daughter and me. Despite so many bumps in the road, things were looking up for me. I would have the life I dreamed of. So why on earth was God necessary in all of this? Still, even though I didn't feel I needed God, I wrote Him a letter one night, during my last semester of school. I asked Him to send me a husband who would be an amazing father to Kiera, generous, funny, kind and handsome. I put that letter away and did not find it until years later.

If I am honest, which is my intent with you, I will admit that even though I had steps in place for a great life, there were areas of lack for sure. I could not have a healthy relationship with a man. It would always end badly. My strategy was to keep getting back out there and trying again no matter what. My measurement of a good weekend was based on whether I had gone out and how many phone numbers I had amassed. I was always around people but still lonely. I had stuff but I still felt empty, prompting me to just pursue more. Something was missing and I was not doing a good job of finding it. My mother was fighting for me in the spirit without me even knowing. I am sure that my mother's intercession for me, her singlehanded prayers as well as those with her new church friends were mostly why I could sense my plan wasn't panning out as I had hoped. She could see I needed the Savior when I simply chose not to. As far as I was concerned, I did not need God; I needed a man to round out the vision I had for my life. This was the last ingredient needed. So, I went to church purely for the reasons mentioned above (insert heavy eye roll).

Despite the defenses I put up, church was actually enjoyable for me. The pastor of the church seemed like a relatable person and not some pompous tyrant who condemned me. He broke down the Bible in a way that was clear to me. On top of that, the music was absolutely soul-stirring. Having grown up singing, and with a deep love for music, I was always transported by the harmonies and powerful lyrics sung by the choir. I was often brought to tears by the beauty of it...on the down-low, of course. I began paying more attention. I felt a desire to experience this again and again. I kept going back. Of course, I wasn't ready to be like one of those "church people".

To me, if you were a full-out Christian, it had to mean you had no sense of humor, lived a perfect life and were judgmental. Christians probably also did not dance, which was a definite necessity in my life—especially a good salsa. No, I could not be a full-out

Christian. However, every Sunday, when the altar call was made, the faintest idea would spring up and move from my mind to flutters in my heart, indicating that I should go down there. I envisioned myself walking down the aisle and I would quickly shut those thoughts down, thinking that I could not bear the change that would come with moving on this impulse. Besides, I got saved at church camp every year for four years straight. I was covered! I would go back to my Monday through Saturday night life where God was politely left on the shelf until the next Sunday morning. By no means was I going to make the walk of shame all the way down the aisles of the church to the altar so everyone could see I was vulnerable. The thought of being on display like that terrified me and kept me glued to my seat for months. However, the inkling, the stirring, grew stronger and stronger as I became more aware of the hole in my soul that no parties, flings, shopping excursions, or friends could fill.

I remember being at home one day and suddenly feeling I could no longer avoid it. The next Sunday, I would have to go up and give my life to the Lord during the altar call. I didn't fight it

> He did not do an instant replay of my most shameful moments or make a list of demands of things I would need to change effective immediately. It was only about love, grace and acceptance.

this time; I just felt resolute that this would be it. I didn't care who was looking or what they were thinking, I was ready for this. That Sunday, I sat on the main level with my mom and my uncle. Yes, no one was safe from my mother's evangelistic fervor—even my extended family! I sat there so eager for the end of service, knowing I would make my way down the aisle and finally do what I knew God had been drawing me toward for months. It was definitely going to go down.

Right after praise and worship, the Pastor got this pensive look on his face, paused momentarily and said, "This week, we are going to do things a little differently, we are going to have the altar call now instead of at the end of service…"

My heart fluttered. That was my heavenly cue. He barely got the sentence out of his mouth before I was hurriedly making my way over everyone in my row and practically running down the aisle to the altar. My mother sobbed from her seat and I don't know if she was shocked or knew all along that her prayers would be answered. God was calling me and I could no longer ignore his call on my heart. He wouldn't even make me wait until the end of service! It was like we both couldn't wait for that moment, me and God. Funny enough, my walk was not a walk of shame. I saw no one around me. No one else mattered. Even after all the boyfriends and flings I had in my life up to that point, I had never felt as wanted as I did by God as I walked down that aisle. He was not pointing out my failures or bad choices. He did not do an instant replay of my most shameful moments or make a list of demands of things I would need to change effective immediately. It was only about love, grace and acceptance.

After the prayer, I was given a Bible and taken to pray with someone. From there, I joined a small group for a membership class led by the Pastor's wife. Later that afternoon at home, I remember opening and reading the Bible for the first time since I was twelve years old. I remember knowing that God saw me—with all of the millions and billions of people in His creation, He saw *me* and wooed *me*, even though I had rejected Him for so long. My mother's prayers were answered.

FOOD *for* THOUGHT:

"But God demonstrates his own love for us in this: While we were still sinners, Christ died for us." (Romans 5:8 NIV)

- Is God wooing and are you receptive? Has shame, fear or anxiety held you back from taking the plunge and saying "Yes, to Jesus?"
- Are you feeling discouraged because it seems as if the more you pray for a loved one, the further they are from God? Trust God and keep praying.

CHAPTER *Two*

I WOULD NEVER...BUT I DID ANYWAY

I would love to say that when I answered God's call on my life, I immediately turned away from all sin and followed him wholeheartedly. However, walking—or in my case, running—to the altar is just the first step in a lifetime marathon. It doesn't always instantly heal all of the broken places, inject us with knowledge of every scripture, or automatically break long-time struggles. Our walk takes work and I wasn't necessarily feeling up to putting my energy toward that. I still needed to work toward my life goals. My husband was not going to just find himself!

It was October 2000, the fall after my college graduation and I was working as an administrative assistant. In my spare time, I would peruse social websites. These sites were the predecessors of Facebook and My Space, if you even remember what that was. My favorite sites were BlackPlanet.com and MiGente.com. Google it, if you must, but it was a big deal at that time. These were not necessarily share-what-you-ate or pictures-of-your-last-vacation type of sites. People were on the prowl for the most part. They'd design pages using actual coding and put up pictures of themselves, often scanned from prints. Those who were really tech savvy would have music playing on their profiles. I wasn't one of those people; the highlight of my page was a picture of me with a midriff top facing a wall and turned to show off my backside and lower back tattoo. Yes, I have a lower back tattoo. I got it during a tattoo party at a friend's dorm room. The artist was surprisingly professional and sanitary despite the fact that at least four of us were getting tattoos in a dorm room. If you want, you can add my tattoo to the list of reasons why God should not have blessed me. The more reasons, the better the glory He gets at the end!

Anyhow, you can guess the kind of attention I was getting with my midriff and my back tattoo on display for the internet, and what I hoped was my future husband to behold. Sometimes, I would interact with people that I knew, but mostly it was strangers who would check out my page and comment or hit on me. Real talk—I loved the attention. I loved compliments and affirmations because they somehow made me feel I was worthy. If a random guy thought I was attractive, then surely the man for me was out there and would think the same. One guy I met on Black Planet had a particularly cocky way about him that appealed to me. He seemed to have a lot of "friends" and set his attention toward me. Based on his popularity and self-proclaimed qualities, the thrill of catching the uncatchable drew me in. He said he was twenty-four years old and single, from the Bronx. We chatted back and forth for a few days and he asked me to go out on that Friday. I agreed.

The night of our date, he pulled up in front of my building in his SUV with the music blasting. It had to be after 10 pm. He was late. He was wearing a fitted baseball cap backwards with the edge right down to his eyes. He had on a jersey (I can't remember what team, maybe the NY Giants), a chain with a huge cross and several chunky gold bracelets. Flashy for sure. I distinctly remember getting into his car and him giving me a once over with his small eyes.

"What's up Miss," he said, with no apology for his tardiness. Then he pulled off and as he turned the corner of my block, I thought, *Yeah, this is the first and last date with this guy.* Have you ever just gotten a vibe from someone right away that put you off? That was what I got from this guy. I edged ever more closely to my side of the car as he sped downtown, crestfallen that he wasn't what I had hoped.

We went to South Street Seaport and got something to eat. We sat in an open court area inside and every five minutes, his Nextel two-way phone (it was a phone that also had a walkie talkie feature) would chirp from one of his friends or his brother. He would answer and just talk about our date right in front of me.

"Yeah, she's cute, heh heh heh."

I was not amused at all. The conversation was very surface as I found myself trying to find things we had in common. He found my having a college degree and being in a sorority to be a bit bourgeois, although I wasn't sure why that was a big deal. He told me he worked for a public utility and made six figures with overtime. He lived in the Bronx with his grandmother and had two kids with his childhood sweetheart. They were no longer together but he supported them and his kids were the apple of his eye.

Well, that was commendable…and we were both parents—that was a commonality. That's pretty much where it ended. Well, we also both had tattoos. I saw a couple of them when he lifted his forearms to show me how he had "Bling Bling" tattooed on either side. So, that's what we'll call him—, Mr. Bling Bling.

After the disaster of a first date (which he thought was a great time), he dropped me at home and I mentally crossed him off of the Mr. Right list. A few days passed and I did not contact him. That was my way of letting him down easily. That Wednesday, he called me right as I was leaving work.

Mr. Bling Bling: "What's up Miss? How you been?"

Me: "Fine thanks."

Mr. Bling Bling: "So when we gonna chill again?"

Me: "Weellll, I don't think that's such a good idea. I mean, you're a nice guy and everything but I don't think we really hit it off."

Mr. Bling Bling: "What? Awww, come on don't tell me that. I really like you."

Me: "Thanks but, I'm good."

Mr. Bling Bling: "Listen, just give me one chance. That's all I'm asking for, just one chance. As a matter of fact, let me pick you up from work and drive you home…"

And that my friend, was how the compromise began. Have you ever read the story in Genesis 25 about Esau and how he gave up his inheritance for a bowl of stew? Jacob and Esau were twin brothers born to Isaac and Rebecca. Esau was the oldest based on birth order. As the oldest, Esau was the brother who would receive his father's blessing and larger inheritance. Well, through some scheming on the part of Jacob and his mom, who really wanted that blessing and birthright for Jacob, they caught Esau in a situation where he had an overwhelming immediate desire to be satiated. Esau was super hungry! Well, how convenient, Jacob had a nice hearty bowl of stew waiting to take his brother's hunger pains away. What did he want in exchange? Just Esau's birthright. It sounds good and crazy to think that someone would actually forsake what would clearly be better in the long term for what looks or feels good at the moment. But forsake it was exactly what Esau did. In that moment, a far off inheritance paled in comparison to stew that would provide immediate satisfaction. Esau compromised. One definition of the word compromise is to make a dishonorable or shameful concession. I don't know what was going through Esau's mind but for me, I did not think about any decision I was making as being dishonorable or shameful. My compromise was not all in one moment, it built over time. However, it started with that momentary decision to seek immediate comfort rather than the delayed gratification that exercising wisdom often brings.

For an opportunity to not have to take an hour-long subway ride, I shut up the voice that told me so clearly that this guy was bad news. Fast forward a few weeks and Mr. Bling Bling was my one and only boo. I know, I can't believe it either. But I mean, he was charming and thought so highly of me and in a sense, he was successful and didn't mind I had a child. I had been apartment-hunting before I met him and found an apartment that happened to be in his complex, so I also was scheduled to move right to his neighborhood. How convenient!

I never visited him. I was never invited and didn't feel the need to since he was over at my place all of the time. He never stayed over or stayed too late though. Not that I didn't want him to, but he said that he wasn't ready to take that step. Mind you, all other "steps" had long been taken, if you catch my drift. All of the things that had so appalled me on our first date became endearing as my discernment became clouded with infatuation. This guy really liked me, I was always hanging out with him and his friends. We would take rides on his motorcycle, which made me feel so cute. He always took me out and I never spent a dime. By that February, we went on a vacation to Puerto Rico together. As long as I didn't try and picture what the long-term future looked like, I could stay enchanted in my present circumstance.

> Our downfalls can be some of the most fun times of our life. That is, until he gets us where he wants us. Then the veil is lifted and we realize we've been in a pig pen the whole time, not a palace.

Also, I had decided I would do things differently this time. I would be an emotionally low-key girlfriend and not a needy annoying one. Mr. Bling Bling did not believe in marriage and I was enough of a cool girl-friend not to broach the subject. I was even cool with him checking out other women and making comments to me. After all, it was only talk and I was too cool to be one of those jealous girls. I figured, as we women often do, that even though this man clearly told me that he was not interested in marriage, that I would somehow fix and change him. None of the rules would apply to me. I would be the game changer for him.

Later that year, we hung out with his son and my daughter who were close in age. I was falling for this guy. So hard that I ignored hints of something lurking all along. You see, when something is taking you down, the enemy will make you feel like you are actually going up. Our downfalls can be some of the most fun times of our life. That is, until he gets us where he wants us. Then the veil is lifted and we realize we've been in a pig pen the whole time, not a palace.

The no-sleep-over rule was one thing, and like I said, I decided to take it as a level of chivalry. I decided to *see* it that way, not that it made sense, mind you. When we were in PR, I looked at his license and saw that he wasn't twenty-four, but thirty years old. He explained that he was meaning to tell me his real age but he didn't want to lose me because I would think he was too old. I let it go. He would do anything to have my love, I decided. Then there were the times when he would kind of disappear and not return my calls or texts for hours or a day. He told me he was visiting his kids and didn't hear his phone. *This kind of devoted father is just the type of man I need in my life*, I decided.

Then there was the fact that none of my friends liked him and thought I was selling myself short. But, what did they know? I was happy for once and not on the receiving end of heartbreak. They'd warm up to him. They didn't know him the way I did, I decided. I felt like I was really in control and too cool to get my heart broken again. I decided to ignore the warnings. The one undeniable red flag came on a morning in late August. Well, it was less of a red flag and more of a red slap across my face. I had just started a job as a teacher and was setting up my classroom in preparation for the school year. My phone rang with his number and when I picked up, a woman said "Lydia?" Hmm, a woman? I decided it was likely his grandmother or mom wanting to finally meet me.

Me: "Yes, who is this?"

Her: "This is Lisette (totally not her real name), Bling Bling's baby's mother. This #@*$ has been lying to you. He lives with me and his two kids. I have pictures of you guys from Puerto Rico and he has been playing you all along."

My sweet reader, did you see this coming, because I absolutely did not! At that moment, my head began to spin. What was I hearing? This did not make sense. This is not what he told me. We had been together for months. How could this be?

Lisette: "Hello, hello? Do you hear me? You need to leave him; he is a lying…"

He must have grabbed the phone from her because the next thing I heard was him saying, "She's crazy Lydia, she's lying. Don't pay her any mind". I hoped with all I had in me that he was right. That she was just a crazy jealous ex who wanted to try and take away the happiness that we had found. I needed to know the truth. She got the phone back from him and he left the house. She asked me to meet her that afternoon so that we could confront him and I agreed.

That afternoon, I met her in front of her mother's building, which, wouldn't you know, was in the same complex that I lived in. I wasn't sure if I should be afraid or angry, and I was honestly both. Who knew if this woman would attack me or not? My confusion about the whole situation trumped my fears, and finally she came outside and walked right up to me. Apparently, she had seen pictures of me so she knew what I looked like. She was beautiful, tall and gorgeous bone structure. Those were my first thoughts. She didn't look much older than I was. She told me she was expecting him any minute and we would surprise him and confront him together. All I could do was keep marveling at the fact that this was really happening. This kind of drama I never would have imagined for myself was unfolding right before me.

A few moments later, I saw his truck coming up the block and when he saw me standing there with her, he accelerated as if he would keep driving. Then he finally slowed down and Lisette told me to get in the back of the car. Side note—*I would not recommend anyone ever getting into a car with a lying man and a scorned, angry woman—especially if you are the reason she is scorned. When I reflect on my life, I recognize these as the "if not for the Grace of God" moments. I have seen too many episodes of Snapped to take for granted that things could have gone south really quickly and I would have been found at the bottom of the Bronx River—but God! Praise break—Thank you Lord for protecting me from my own foolish decisions, thank you so much Lord!*

Anyhow, I digress—so I got into the back of the car and Lisette got into the passenger seat. The passenger seat where I used to put my feet up on the dashboard, the one where I sat as Bling Bling would sing me love songs in a silly voice, where he would caress my cheek as he drove. Where we kissed after each date. That seat was never mine and I sat there in the back seat, feeling belittled, stupid and awkward. There wasn't too much time for self-reflection though because Ms. Lisette quickly tore into Mr. Bling Bling!

Lisette: "Tell her the truth @%&*...tell her who you live with. Tell her!"

Mr. Bling Bling: Silence

Lisette: "Tell her because if you don't I will!"

Mr. Bling Bling: "You..."

Lisette: "Say it louder, tell the truth for once!"

Mr. Bling Bling: "With you alright, I live with you, are you happy now?"

There was something about hearing it come from his own mouth that jolted me from my state of shock to utter anger.

As the words were leaving his mouth, I finally began crying and the jilted woman in me screamed, "Why? Why would you lie to me like that?" He didn't have an answer for me. He kept driving aimlessly around as Lisette and I took turns screaming at him. My phone kept ringing. I was supposed to have been somewhere that afternoon and didn't even call to cancel. Kiera was at my mother's house and that was as far as I prepared. I was wrapped up in this drama that didn't exist a few hours ago, and now it was all I could think about.

Lisette: "Do you love her? Tell me?"

Mr. Bling Bling: "Yes I do, and I have a much better time with her than I do with you, but I'm not leaving my kids."

Lisette started crying. I felt like dirt under a shoe. But something about hearing him SAY he loved me somehow made me feel I hadn't completely lost. By this point, we were in front of my building—she now knew where I lived.

Lisette: "Now you know what he is. But he is mine, we have kids and he is mine."

Me: "I don't ever want to see you again, you disgust me."

At that I got out of the car and hurried to my apartment.

What do you do when you are in shock and pain? I called my mom who came over and just held me as I cried uncontrollably. I spent the next couple of days swollen-eyed, chain smoking and miserable. The only prayer I thought to mutter was, "God, make it stop hurting". Graciously, none of my friends gave me an I-told-you-so; just support.

If only I had ridden out that pain, changed my number and moved on. U*mmm, didn't you?* you're probably asking. I wish I could tell you that's what I did, but after a few days, he called. He pleaded, apologized, said all of the things that I wanted to hear—everything except that he was going to leave Lisette and be with me. It was because of his kids, he told me. So, in an effort not to look like a complete ninny, I slowly agreed that we would be together but I would be free to see other people. That way I didn't feel I was giving in completely. I still had some of that "control"—which, real talk, I never had. Now that we were seeing each other again, we would have to sneak around because Lisette had friends who would keep an eye on my building and call her if Bling Bling was ever seen going in or coming out. I also kept our reconciliation a secret from my friends and family who never liked him to begin with. So now I was sneaking around and waiting on a man who I knew was with someone else. If I could go back in time, I would find myself and give myself a good shaking. But at the time, I felt that any time with the man I wanted to be with was enough. Even though there were countless nights now when he wouldn't show up for our plans at all and wouldn't answer my calls.

As a way to try and numb the pain, I began having Bacardi Limon every night after putting Kiera to bed, to help me fall asleep. Then, to save face and divert my attention, I started dating other guys. That way, I would never have to be alone on a Friday night when Kiera was with my parents, regardless of Bling Bling. I honestly can't even remember most of the names of the guys that I dated during that time, but I knew that I just couldn't be alone. Weekends were for dating and partying in my book and if that wasn't happening, then I felt like I was missing out on living. However, I will say there were some nice young men with potential who pursued me that I treated poorly because I wanted what I could not have. I was still going to church most Sundays. Even though I was there physically, my mind was often elsewhere and I was not connected.

Being connected, in my opinion, meant becoming one of the perfect church people and I certainly could never be one of those, especially since this fiasco. So, despite the fact that I was almost two years into attending church, I was sliding deeper into a pit of self-destruction without realizing it.

I remember one night in particular when I had asked my mom to babysit my daughter. I told her I was hanging out with some friends, when in actuality I was meeting Bling Bling. We were riding on his motorcycle that night and I remember burning my leg on the exhaust pipe of his bike while dismounting. A week or so later, I was at a family event and my aunt, who was a NYC police officer, was there. She and my mom were talking and she casually asked me, "what happened to your leg?"

"Oh, nothing, I burnt it with the iron," I quickly replied.

"It looks like a motorcycle burn to me," she said. She then casually turned to my mother and they exchanged a knowing glance. That you-cannot-fool-a-mother glance. She likely had seen

> God had never left me and He wasn't mad at me. As a matter of fact, He was sending his other children in my path to help lead me back. Unlike Esau, I had not lost everything.

me and reported this to my mom whose suspicions I was again entwined with Mr. Bling Bling were then confirmed. Regardless of how they knew, I felt embarrassed, silly and ashamed. I was an adult and had been sneaking around in an unhealthy, unfruitful relationship. How was this ever going to lead to what I wanted in life? It wasn't, and I had to count my losses and accept it. But it was hard to follow through on what I knew I needed to do.

By what could only be classified as Divine grace, I was laid off from my job as a teacher and had to move out of my apartment and back with my parents while I got financially stable again. So, physically, I was out of the situation. I started waitressing at a local restaurant and focusing more on a singing group I was a part of. Although I was sad and feeling rejected, I slowly began moving on from Mr. Bling Bling emotionally and mentally, and being out of the vicinity where it all took place was a big help. Although I was one toe in the church, my singing group, Soul Tres, was having our songs arranged by one of the Assistant Pastors at my church who was really musically gifted and directed the choir that I loved so much. Even though the three of us in Soul Tres—myself, Selina, a close friend of mine since middle school and Tracy, our friend from college—were not typical church girls, Pastor Bobby started each rehearsal with prayer and spoke encouragement and blessings into our lives with no judgement. God had never left me and He wasn't mad at me. As a matter of fact, He was sending his other children in my path to help lead me back. Unlike Esau, I had not lost everything. There was still hope if I would let go of what I thought I could not live without. But it would take some time.

One afternoon, I was in my mom's kitchen when Bling Bling called from a private number. He said he missed me, he knew we would be together again and asked me to reconsider because he loved me. I calmly told him that his love was just not enough. No, we would not be getting back together. He should stop trying. I finally closed the door I never should have opened years prior.

FOOD *for* THOUGHT:

"No temptation has overtaken you except what is common to mankind. And God is faithful; he will not let you be tempted beyond what you can bear. But when you are tempted, he will also provide a way out so that you can endure it."

(1 Corinthians 10:13 NIV)

- Are there any areas of your life where you are being tempted to compromise? If so, identify them.
- What are some of the ways God has provided a way out of compromising situations?

CHAPTER *Three*

HIGHER EDUCATION

*I*n 2002, I got a job at The King's College, a Christian College that was located in the Empire State Building at the time. My position was in the Admissions Department. This was not a job of my choosing. I had been laid off at my last position, which resulted in my moving back home with my parents and needing full-time work. Through the senior pastor of my church and, likely, my mother's fervent prayers again, I interviewed for and was offered this job. A job I did not want. Firstly, I did not want to work around a bunch of stuffy old Christians, and secondly, College Admissions seemed to me to be competitive and numbers driven and not at all what I wanted for a career. Essentially, I felt in no way qualified either spiritually or professionally, to be a part of this team. But I took the job because no other jobs were panning out, and also because I knew there was a direct and crucial correlation between steady employment and moving back into my own place. I really wanted to be back in my own place.

I really did not know what to expect at my new job. Would these all be uptight, perfect people who would look down on me? Would I know how to speak "Christianese"? I really was not that familiar with the Bible, so would that be an issue? What benchmarks would I have to hit in order to keep my job? There were so many ways for this to be an epic fail and I had mentally entertained each one in painstaking detail on that initial subway ride down to my demise—I mean, my new job. I took the elevator down to the basement level (quite an anti-climactic location for working in the Empire State Building) and stepped out into what looked like the authentic interior of a modern college administration building. I was greeted warmly by the receptionist who was also a student, and then by my new boss, Brian Bell.

Brian, the Director of Admissions, was an uber cheerful, down-to-earth thirty-something who really, really loved Jesus, his family, his job and The King's College. Like, *a lot*. Brian had graduated from King's years before, and it seemed getting to work there was like the fulfillment of a dream for him. Well, that made one of us. He was married with two small children who would often come by to visit him at the office. His wife was just as sweet as he was and their children were beyond cute and well-behaved. If I remember correctly, and I'm pretty sure I do, the Bell family either did not own a television or their children had never seen a television except to watch Veggie Tales on VHS. I felt like I was meeting characters out of some work of fiction in real life. But this was not fiction—these people were real, and not only real, but genuine. They were genuine and welcoming which helped to ease the feeling of inferiority moving through me.

Brian was very sensitive to my newness to all of it and helped me recognize the gifts that God had placed in me and how they could be used at this job. For instance, guiding tours was a part of the job I thrived in because I had studied acting and it was like giving a performance with the addition of being agile, and also improvising, depending on what questions were asked or who happened to be hanging around the student common area.

Brian patiently explained a lot of things to me about God and college admissions without judgment. Once we were hosting a group of perspective students from a more charismatic denomination than I was accustomed to. At the end of our meeting, we bowed our heads for prayer and instead of one person solemnly addressing God, every single person started passionately and personally praying out loud all at once. My head shot up in shock, not knowing what to think, and as I glanced around, I saw Brian chuckle at me and put his head back down. I smirked awkwardly and quickly put my head back down, trying to weave together a sentence from the threads of different voices. Afterwards, he told me he knew I'd be taken aback by this different type of prayer which was why he was humored. I was tickled by how it happened as well, but I was more so very intrigued with experiencing prayer and worship with other kinds of Christians.

They weren't even from across the country or anything either— they were from the Bronx! Because my job required that I attend college fairs and church events to recruit students, I spent a lot of time visiting churches throughout New York City. Working at King's was like taking a class in different Christian cultures and learning that for everything that seemed so different, they were just regular people like me. It was at these times that I began to explore my own worship. At my own church, I often felt out of place and unsure of how to communicate with God through worship. Some people raised their hands, and of course, there was clapping, but for the most part, it was conservative.

While at King's, I visited churches with dynamic youth nights where young people—who looked so much cooler and relevant than I did—worshipped God with reckless abandon, without frilly language or lofty prayers. They exclaimed that they loved Him and pleaded that they needed him, no matter who was within ear shot. They danced, waved their hands, and sobbed, and it did not matter who was around. I thought, what if I gave in like that when I felt God's love and grace overwhelming me? What if I spoke to God out loud and had real talk and didn't care who heard? In these other churches, where I could be more anonymous, I began to enjoy praise and worship not only as a spectator, envious and in awe of how people could commune with God, but as a participant, and I did not feel completely awkward and out of place. What I experienced Monday through Friday at

> *Slowly but surely, I was opening up to the possibility that people from church were nothing to be intimidated by. Maybe they were just as normal and yes, flawed as the God-loving people I worked with. Maybe you could love God and be in relationship with Him and still have a sense of humor and flaws.*

King's had a huge impact on my Sunday life. Slowly but surely, I was opening up to the possibility that people from church were nothing to be intimidated by. Maybe they were just as normal and yes, flawed as the God-loving people I worked with. Maybe you could love God and be in relationship with Him and still have a sense of humor and flaws.

The rest of the admissions team were also from various walks of life. Cheryl was a former professional ballroom dancer from California. She was a couple of years into her relationship with God and was as authentically sunny and warm as the state she hailed from. We would go on regular trips to the bathroom together, just like women for ages have done as a form of bonding, and she would tell me about her Christian boyfriend and how he was so different than any other man she had ever dated. Their pastimes included attending small group at their church and praying together. As much as I wanted to write it all off as corny and void of fun, there were also stories of their latest romantic (and still really PG rated) dates and of his latest chivalrous gestures. Now, those were things I could possibly get with.

Then there was James from Queens, born and raised in the Lord but still so New York! James was the youngest of us all and was married with dreams of being a missionary and pastor. Although he was younger than me, he took on a big brother role, which was comforting. Stephanie, a single mom like me, had one of the gentlest and most generous spirits I have ever known. You couldn't compliment anything of hers without it then becoming a gift to you.

Omar was also young and married, a hardcore example of faith, and really on fire for God. Our student aid was Cecilia from Peru, a young woman who was very even-keeled and often seemed more mature than most of us. These people loved the Lord but were not pretentious or judgmental. I thought they would see me, hear the things I said, take note of my naiveté and write me off or, at the very least, be patronizing. I was wrong. I was welcomed to the team and enjoyed our combination of playful banter and spiritual discourse over the cubicle walls. I could ask my colleagues questions I couldn't exactly raise my hand to ask during service, and that alone helped me to understand God and the Bible. We started staff meetings with prayer and shared encouragement, scriptures and devotions regularly. When we had goals, fulfilling them was not just based on our skills and talent but we asked God for His direction and favor over the work of our hands—a concept I was not used to. I always thought I had to do everything on my own, especially work assignments. Now I was learning that God cared about all aspects of my life and was willing and able to help me with everything.

My time at King's also gave me a fresh look into love and marriage, follower-of-Jesus style. Cheryl was candid that she and her beau were waiting until marriage to be physical. This sounded completely unnecessary and torturous to me but I could not deny that she had a special relationship and was treated well. Brian, James and Omar were all married and often talked about their wives and home life. Here were these relatively young men who loved their wives, respected them and had appropriate boundaries with others and served their families. At many places I worked, some married men would complain about their wives and have inappropriately close relationships with women at work whom they would deem "work wives". I also, unfortunately, had married men come on to me numerous times in my career. On the flipside, my colleagues at King's exuded enthusiasm, even gratefulness, about being married. Marriage was cool for them. Not many young men I had known had the same sentiment. In this circle, a woman's virtue seemed at least something to be valued. In my past experience, virtue was perceived as juvenile, and being sexual and not married was both cosmopolitan and expected.

Now, let me say this and please understand me clearly. I do not have these people, or Christians in general, on a pedestal. Infidelity, strife, betrayal and everything in between do happen in both Christian and secular marriages alike. Every marriage has valleys and peaks and no one except Jesus Himself is perfect. I didn't see perfection at my job, I saw people, regular people, who lived out in front of me what it was like to be engaged in a relationship with God. Perfection (feigned perfection) would have scared me away. A group of people who just followed rules to feel like they earned their place in God would have miseducated me. God had me in that particular place, with those particular people, for that particular season. It was as though He wanted to introduce me to His other children that He knew I'd get along really well with.

In developing rapport with my colleagues, I was drawn to wanting more of a rapport with God. He was still incessantly wooing me and I like to think that He was removing options so I had to pay attention. Prior to this job, I hadn't been seeking God in my spare time. God time was Sunday from noon to 1:30. *Punto, finito.* I was still trying to make what I wanted happen in my own way and timing. So, what happened? I ended up with a job where I was spending most of my work days, so many hours of my life, with God and people who really loved Him. He was seeking me and I was intrigued to start really seeking Him.

I think back now about how much I did NOT want to be a college admissions counselor, how I did NOT want to work for a Christian company, let alone be all up in churches for a living. God stood His Holy ground with me. He didn't waiver upon my continual whining and displeasure, as I have done at times as a parent. He also didn't force anything on me because He knew what was good for me, which I have also done as a parent. He merely opened a door I decided to walk through. When I walked in, I was surrounded by love, acceptance and truth. It was then up to me to choose whether I wanted to delve deeper in Him or stay where I was. I decided to stop dipping my toes in and out and put both feet in the water. But, I was still in the shallow end of the pool.

FOOD *for* THOUGHT

- What preconceived notions have held you back from authentically connecting with others? Could those notions be wrong?

- Where is God leading you, but you have been resistant? Consider this: *Maybe the place you are resisting is the very place you should be.*

CHAPTER Four

SO CLOSE, YET SO FAR

The more I gleaned at work and learned about the way God desired for us to engage romantically, the weirder I would feel about my own casual dating. During my early days at King's, I dated around unsuccessfully until, finally, I started seeing someone casually. I'd go over to his place mostly on nights when I would leave the nightclub feeling unwanted, lonely and powerless. There were no dates with this guy. There was no wooing. There was a phone call, a cab ride, an encounter and me getting home shortly before sunrise.

After a couple of months of this, I realized that, not only was my loneliness not being relieved, but I also didn't feel good about what I was doing. I started feeling remorseful and lost, and if I am honest, I felt a little shameful too. There was no love; there wasn't even infatuation. There was a mutual understanding and though I felt physically desired by this guy, it just was not enough. It wasn't worth the cab fare or the lingering emptiness. I was disobedient to God but I didn't want to be flagrantly so. I began thinking, "Maybe there was a chance for me to have what my friends at work had. Maybe I could be like Cheryl and have my life change and have an amazing Christian man who loved me." It was a long shot, but at the very least I knew this current situation wasn't cool with me anymore. So, I ended it. Without a trace of tears, sadness or remorse on either of our parts. I was still a mess, but casual sex was one vice that didn't even feel good anymore. Maybe, I thought, I was worth more. Maybe someone else would see that.

Even with all of my observing, learning and growing, I still had my Mi Gente social media account and would check my page occasionally just to stay in the know. One day, there was a message from someone whose profile name was Gregluva. I couldn't judge—my profile name was Pink Panther. As a matter of fact, don't you go judging either. Those were the days when no one used their real name in their email or social media. Gregluva's real name was Greg and I vaguely remembered him from my college days. He went to another school on Long Island and had friends and frat brothers at my school, so he was often at my campus for parties and events. I even dated one of his friends in my freshman year and recall a brief mention of Gregluva. I then promptly forgot all about him. I can honestly say I never paid any attention to this guy when I was in school. He may as well have been wallpaper.

But that day when I read his message, "Just saying hi", and looked at his profile picture, standing casually in a black tank top, tall and muscular and so gosh darned handsome, I wondered why I hadn't paid attention before. No matter, he was right before me now and I was paying attention! We exchanged email addresses and spent the next couple of days in polite and semi-flirtatious correspondence. Not only was this guy pretty hot, but I found out he also worked with kids as a social worker. There was a beautiful brain in that beautiful head and a heart in that chiseled chest. Alright now! He asked me out on a date for that Friday. I tried to act like I needed to look at my calendar and waited a bit before replying, but in my mind, I was screaming YES!!!!

That evening is still vivid in my memory. It was a drizzly spring evening in early May, cool but pleasant. I could smell a mix of the rain and his cologne as we shared an umbrella and walked from his car to a small Italian restaurant on Second Avenue in Manhattan. At 6'2, he towered almost a foot over me, even with my heels on. I remember feeling safe and giddy and trying really hard not to let any of it show. The restaurant was intimate and candlelit, perfect for lingering gazes and conversation. Greg had joined a fraternity in college that focused on uplifting and educating men of color and was very well versed on the topic of African American and Latino history. While I had studied African American history and read books on the Black and Latino experience in America, I was nowhere near Greg's level of passion and knowledge. So, over fettuccine and chicken parmesan, he talked to me about the African Diaspora, how school textbooks don't tell the whole story and how I should get Kiera a copy of "A People's History of the United States". Was he really giving me a reading list for my daughter on our first date?! He was so socially conscious, eloquent and intelligent that I could hardly stand it—and he had a great sense of humor to boot!

As he spoke, I thought, *Oh gorgeous man sitting across the table from me, where have you been all of my life? I will obtain and read every social-ly-conscious book you recommend and we will have long, deep socially-conscious conversations as we gaze longingly into each other's eyes forever and ever, Amen.* It felt like no one else was on the streets and we floated back to his car after dinner.

At the end of the date, we sat outside of my building and I waited for him to lean in and kiss me. Instead he just said goodnight and gave me a side hug. What in the world? This is not how an engaging, intellectually and physically electric date ends! I was surprised and tried to figure out what I had misinterpreted. I thought our date went great and I had never in life had a great date that did not end with a kiss. I went inside, got Kiera from my mom's house and went up to my apartment where my roommate and a couple of our friends were hanging out.

"So how was your date?", she asked. Just as I was about to answer, my cell phone rang. It was Greg.

I tried to sound cool, "Hey, what's up?"

"I just wanted to let you know I had a really, really good time," he said in his deep, velvety voice.

"Really, then why didn't you kiss me?" I asked, trying to sound unbothered, not very convincingly.

"Because, it was our first date and I want to be respectful."

At this, my heart did a triple backflip and stuck a landing so hard that a swarm of butterflies took off flying from the pit of my belly all the way up my spine and out of the top of my head.

We talked all night. I am not exaggerating—all...night...long.

We talked about our favorite foods, our childhoods, college days and who we knew in common. And yes, as the sun rose and we knew it was time to get off of the phone, we had a lengthy exchange of the tried and true, "you hang up first" exchange. That one never gets old. I was smitten. And so was Greg. For the next few weeks, we were all but inseparable. Our connection was at almost every level. We had similar upbringings, similar interests and senses of humor. We both loved the Lord of the Rings movies. The nerd in me connected with the nerd in him. Bliss. A few weeks in, I introduced him to Kiera, something I very rarely did. I read a couple of books from his list to which he seemed impressed. He took Kiera and me to wait in line for the latest Harry Potter book to be released. We were having a great time.

One thing we did not have in common was an interest in God. Greg knew I was a Christian, but religion had never been a significant topic of conversation. I only knew that he had grown up going to church with his mom and then stopped as a teenager. To be honest, I didn't want to push too hard. I just knew that I was on the cusp of having one of my heart's desires filled in record time, so I didn't want to rock the boat too hard. One evening, the conversation found its way to the topic of physical intimacy and I decided to go ahead and stand for righteousness. My friends at work were really rubbing off

> *"I'm a Christian so I don't sleep with anyone right away, only after a couple of months." Man, I was so proud making that declaration.*

on me. So, I said to Greg, with beaming confidence and a little bit of pride, "I'm a Christian so I don't sleep with anyone right away, only after a couple of months." Man, I was so proud making that declaration. Never mind that it had no basis at all in the Word of God or that it was never how the topic was framed to me by my colleagues. It was what felt right to me at the time. I wanted God; I really did. But my goodness, did I also want Gregluva. So, I tried to make them both fit into my life. Instead of casually dating and being intimate with guys, I thought I was doing God a favor by waiting a couple of months and dating someone seriously before taking that plunge. Meanwhile, God's will for me was to wait until marriage. But, in my mind I thought, what person that has lived a life like mine actually does that? I wasn't chaste or virtuous. The nails had been hammered into that coffin years ago. This was the best I could do and God would understand. In my mind, I was pleasing everyone, but mostly myself. This was progress to me. I was going to church regularly, praying sometimes and I now had Christian colleagues. Surely, all of these good deeds had opened the door for this man to come into my life on my terms. Isn't that the trap we begin entertaining? That we do good deeds and in exchange God gives us blessings? Well, the plunge didn't even take a couple of months, more like weeks. So much for my declaration.

One evening, Greg and I did start talking about religion. My church was having "bring a friend day" and I decided to ask Greg if he wanted to come. Somehow the conversation led to him going on a tangent, albeit an eloquent one, about organized religion.

He asked, "Who's to say the answer is Jesus? What if it's Confucius or Mohammad or Buddha?"

Without pause, I replied, "I don't know about any of that, all I know is that Jesus changed my life."

I know what you are thinking. *Ummm, how changed were you, Miss Couple of Months?* How would this guy believe anything you said about God? What example were you? Yes, I know. But, the truth is, I was changed. I was not the same person I was six months or a year before that. Sure, I had a way to go, but God had begun a work in me. I just fought it a lot. Sometimes, we overthink what goes into sharing the Gospel with people and think that we need to know the Bible by heart, or have gone to seminary, or be those pesky perfect Christians, for people to be moved. That's just not true. Apparently, the Holy Spirit had already been preparing Greg's heart for this moment because I cannot take credit for anything when all I had was a flimsy, yet passionate, response. The only thing I had to do was be bold enough to at least say something.

There it was; for the man who looked at facts, examined truths and treasured information, my ineloquent but heartfelt truth about how God changed my life was enough for him. Greg agreed to come to church that Sunday.

I don't know what I was expecting by having Greg come to church, but when God calls someone, He orchestrates some logistics behind the scenes that we have no idea about. We sat in my usual balcony spot. Kiera sat with us and so did my cousin whom I also invited. My mom sang in the choir and was down below on the main floor. She really liked Greg and was no doubt praying for him to marry and make an honest woman of me. Service was awesome. The praise and worship was captivating, and the sermon, clear, powerful and relatable. In my mind, I thought if nothing else, Greg would have had a pretty good time, but God had something more planned. After the service, we went out to eat and he shared that he really enjoyed the service and would be returning. Cool!

While Greg did begin to attend some church services with me, we didn't change any of our behaviors. He was sleeping over at my place. I would sneak him out in the morning and then he'd come back in as if he were just coming by for breakfast. What a sly one I was. I was living completely out of God's order but didn't feel like I was. That's the thing; I was feeling loved by the Lord and growing in my walk even though I wasn't completely obedient. When you are new in your walk, God doesn't wait for you stop everything cold turkey and then love you—he loves you so much in spite of yourself that you can't help but want to give everything over to Him. But let's not be hasty, I was not there yet. I was enjoying my beau and Jesus, on my own terms. Best of both worlds—but not.

I excitedly shared with my co-workers at Kings that I was dating someone. Cheryl and I had numerous bathroom trips to exchange talk of romantic gestures and dates. James, big brother figure that he was, made sure to ask about this new guy's relationship with the Lord and how well he treated me. I assured him that Greg was coming to church with me and was one of the most respectable and attentive guys I had ever dated. Not only that, but one of our pastors had taken him under his wing and he was meeting other men. Everyone was happy for me. I was happy for me. My dreams were coming true.

Oh, what a beautiful spring and early summer it was. Long walks, laughs, carefree kisses in the park or on subway platforms. Movie nights, cuddling and yes, long gazes. I was really settling in and getting comfortable with thinking that this could actually be it. I wouldn't be hurt like I was before. My time had come.

Well, here's the thing, when you get into God's presence, when you begin to really hear the Word and engage in a relationship with Him, your outlook about some things may change—even if you don't want it to. First, instead of careless pillow talk, a weird guilt started creeping in after our trysts ended. I started to feel like I was sneaking around and it didn't feel good. Before, I just felt like I was being discreet and keeping my business to myself. Now, I felt like I was just being a sneak and letting God and the people who were investing in me down. Then, Greg started to change. For our first couple of months, it was all about me, we saw each other frequently and spoke constantly. Then the three times a day phone calls diminished to calling once a day, and then every other day. I began questioning what I did. Was it because I was a single mom? He had never dated a woman with children before. Was I too clingy? What the heck happened?

One day he called to say he needed to talk. He came by my house and I was in the kitchen, frying plantains and chicken. I kept my eyes on the stove, not knowing what to expect but hoping for the best. Maybe he was coming over to apologize for being so distant and we would embrace, kiss, and go back to the way we were. He was silent for a minute, just watching me cook and looking awkward. Then he explained there was an ex-girlfriend that he was not completely over and that she was back in town. My heart sank and a lump developed in my throat. I swallowed hard and let anger take over so I could hide my hurt under it. Here I was again. What a stupid fool I had been to think I could actually love and be loved in return. I turned the chicken. Over the loud sizzling and popping, Greg ended his explanation by saying he did not want to stop seeing me, but he had a lot to think about. When put into a corner, we sometimes revert to old patterns. Instead of kindly telling him to get out of my house and moving on, I acquiesced. Surely, Greg would choose me. The only sure thing was that I was compromising myself again.

I've kept a journal for much of my life. During this time, what had mainly been musings on life, venting, and the recording of events, became written prayers. I wrote to God about my dreams and hopes, and asked for favor and guidance. I asked Him to help me do what was right in this relationship. I had heard about God's will and how it was best. I asked God for His will. I had hoped that His will was for Greg and me to be together. I couldn't see why it couldn't be.

We continued dating, but there was no change in Greg's distancing behavior toward me; in fact it got worse. He was still attending my church and made friends there. Friends outside of me. I would leave our times together feeling drained, hurt and incomplete. All of this occurred between May and July of that year. As quickly as our romance had ignited, the fire blew out and hard as I tried, I couldn't get it going again.

One night, we were on the phone and I was complaining about how we hadn't seen each other in a few days and asking that classic question, "Where are we in our relationship?" In my frustration, I felt the Lord impressing on me: "Break up with him." Internally, I replied "Lord, please no, we can work this out." He didn't relent. He said, "You deserve better. Stop settling. The one I have for you will love you. There will not be confusion about it and you will not have to chase after him."

With my heart beating so fast, I blurted out, "I deserve to have someone who is crazy about me. I think we should stop seeing each other." In that split second, I was hoping that, faced with this finality, Greg would realize what he would be missing, tell me that he was crazy about me and he was just in a weird place mentally, and drive from his apartment in Brooklyn to mine in East Harlem, to take me into his arms, and kiss me passionately.

Greg replied coolly, "OK."

OK? That was it? Didn't these past few months mean anything? Weren't we so right for each other? This wasn't the response I had wanted, but I couldn't take it back. My voice cracked as I told him to have a good life and hung up. Then I dove face first into my pillow and cried…all night…and called out sick from work the next morning…took Kiera to school, then cried all day. How did I get here again? I was so close, the closest I had ever been, but still not good enough. Heartbreak seemed to be all I was destined for. I cried to God and asked Him why things had to be this way. Why was I again back to square one? I was trying. When I had asked God to help me, I didn't think this was part of the package. This pill was a tough one to swallow, but I would have to. I had been broken hearted before; this was nothing new. Now at least I could ask God to help me heal.

FOOD *for* THOUGHT

"There is a way that appears to be right, but in the end it leads to death."
(Proverbs 14:12 NIV)

- Are you holding on to something (behavior, attitude or lifestyle) or someone that's below God's standard for your life?
- Are you asking God about the choices you are making? How can you begin to involve God in your decision-making process?

PART TWO

Disappointment

CHAPTER *Five*

WHEN IT HURTS SO BAD

Moving on from Greg probably would have been so much easier if not for one detail—he still attended my church. I don't even think that I could call it "my" church anymore since he had begun attending regularly and had made several friends. He had joined the Usher Board and was volunteering with the Youth Ministry. He was more involved than I was! However, for the most part, he would go to the 9am service and I would go to the noon service so I didn't necessarily have to see him every week. When I did see him, we exchanged quick pleasantries and he seemed happy and at peace. No lament, no regrets. Nice. Maybe it was best we went to different services. Out of sight, out of mind, out of heart. That's what I hoped for.

A few weeks after our break up, Greg called me saying he was excited to share news. He told me that at morning service, the Pastor made an altar call asking if anyone would like to accept Christ as their Savior. Like every other week, he sat uncomfortably through this part of the service but this time, there was that call, similar to the one I had experienced, where you feel like that call is exclusively for you and God is calling you at that very moment to become His.

Unlike me, Greg did not go up for the altar call. He stayed seated through the rest of the service and walked out of the church after the benediction. He even walked to his car and all the while, felt something beckoning him back. He shared that as he got to his car and unlocked the door, he could no longer ignore what he needed to do. He went back to the church, found the Pastor and accepted the Lord Jesus as his Savior. Greg was elated as he recounted this story and I was truly happy for him. How wonderful was it that this man who I cared for so very much now had his name written in the Lamb's book of life to join God in Heaven for eternity? Greg shared that he couldn't wait to tell me this news and while that sounded good to hear, I wondered why he even cared whether I knew he was saved or not. He seemed to have moved on just fine from our relationship while I was still secretly licking my wounds. Not only did he have new friends through church, but now he also had a new relationship with Christ. These exciting things happened without me, the person who had invited him to begin with. Regardless of this literally new life without me, we effortlessly spent an hour or so on the phone that day, catching up and enjoying the easy banter that always existed between us.

At the end of our conversation, we decided that although it hadn't worked out romantically, we would be friends. Friends, we would be friends. Honestly, I did not want to be just friends. But if being friends would mean that we'd once again get to hang out, then I would try to stuff my feelings way down and take this offer. Even as I type this, I can't help but sigh at how naïve I was to think that I could be just friends with a man who I had such deep affection for. Especially since the last piece of the puzzle making him an entire catch had now been placed. He was now not only handsome, intelligent, funny, generous and kind but he was also now saved and excited about it! The total package right in front of me and I was willingly ushered into the friend zone with him. As for how I reconciled this with what God had placed on my heart, I reasoned, *God had said break up with him, He didn't say we couldn't be friends, right?* So, I opened the door again, not realizing that trying to be friends would be more than I had bargained for.

This is how the next few months went. Greg would come over to hang out, watch a movie and even pray and study the Bible with me. We would have a grand time in each other's company. There would be laughter, mirth, high-jinx and meaningful conversation. We even took a salsa dance class together along with Selina and some of my other friends. We hung out, he went home, I went home and there was nothing further. Greg was a nightclub promoter as a side hustle (baby steps, don't judge), so I would often recruit my friends and make my way to the club where he worked to get to spend time with, um I mean, to support him.

So, I would be at the club with my girls and would get into Greg's line of sight and try to look like I was having the time of my life. He hardly paid attention. At the end of most of these nights, I would make my way over to say goodbye and we'd share a friendly hug. I would linger a little too long taking in the scent of his cologne and all of my defenses would be disarmed.

"Greg, why can't we be together?" I would ask, as if he was the one who had ended it, as if I hadn't heard God clearly, as if he was even interested in being together. He would sigh and gingerly unravel my arms from around him.

"I don't know, I just don't feel compelled to", he would say. Then he would walk away and I would stand there awkwardly, feeling foolish and heartbroken all over again. Sometimes, we would both add to the confusion by talking about how well we get along. This cruel self-inflicted cycle of hanging and longing continued for months. I was not very good at respecting the friend zone. The more I persisted and communicated my desire for us to be together after we hung out, the farther away he would drift. I don't know why I did this. I had prayed and it seemed God answered me by allowing this relationship to fizzle. While I knew what God said was true, that I deserved better, I didn't believe better would come for me. I had to get what was right in front of me, right then.

> *While I knew what God said was true, that I deserved better, I didn't believe better would come for me. I had to get what was right in front of me, right then.*

The Copacabana, a nightclub on 34th Street, would have after-work Wednesdays that were very popular. Tons of people from young professionals to older seasoned dancers would attend to get their salsa dancing on. I so happened to still be working at The King's College which was a short walk away and would meet my friends there for a couple of hours to enjoy some salsa dancing, unwind, and hopefully bump into Greg who also attended from time to time. My hope? Maybe for him to see me in all of my salsa dancing glory and realize what a catch I was. I mean, who could resist me putting into practice all of those salsa moves we had learned in class? My hope in turning this around was sickeningly relentless.

One night, I spotted Greg at the Copa with a couple of his friends. I immediately found a dance partner, some middle-aged man who smelled of classic Old Spice cologne and had major moves. Old Spice man had me doing double and even triple turns. My shines (the solo moves that you do during salsa) were on-point, a small crowd even gathered around us. I felt like the salsa queen! This was it! The moment that would turn the tide! Surely, my fiery moves were burning straight into Greg's heart leading him to remember what he once found irresistible in me and we would be leaving together. Dance for that man, girl, dance! At the end of the song, my seasoned partner, Old Spice, dipped me dramatically and when I got up again, breathing hard, smiling broadly, sweating and so proud of my performance, I looked around and noticed that Greg was gone. He didn't even stay around for my big finish. Drats! I disappointedly thanked Old Spice and made my way downstairs to the hip-hop room, but he wasn't there. Then on to the reggae room; no Greg either. Even though the night was young, I quickly gathered my friends and made a beeline for the exit.

I spotted him outside walking to his car and ran without looking like I was trying to run to catch up with him.

"Hey, walk with me," I said as I came up from behind and

linked my arm into his. My friends—my poor, loyal friends—trailed behind, probably trying not to be disgusted at my desperation. Greg walked me to a main avenue and when we got there, I thanked him and then went for it yet again. "Kiss me Greg, please," I playfully pleaded as I leaned up to him. He gently but firmly put my hands down and told me to go home and get some rest. Then he walked away. At this point, I know my behavior qualified as insanity. Doing the same thing repeatedly, expecting a different result. I knew better. From the outside in, I knew that I was being "that" girl and I didn't want to be. I was annoying and a bit pathetic. For goodness sake, why wouldn't I take no for an answer? I knew I was failing and I would go home and journal about it and tell myself it was the last time I would be so foolish. Then I'd have another cringe-worthy moment soon after. I knew what God would have to say. He'd want me to walk away and wait on Him. To stop pursuing. Isn't that what He said that night, months ago? Stop pursuing, you will be pursued.

Lest you give up on me and close this book, take heart. This was close to—but not exactly—the point when I finally gathered some dignity and stopped chasing after this man. There were still a couple more moments that I am not too proud of. Not because we compromised physically in any way—things were strictly platonic. My frustration with where I was at that time came from the fact that I would make myself available to hang out and allow myself to be so emotionally vulnerable, knowing I wanted to be more than friends and hoping something would suddenly change in my favor. I did not guard my heart, nor did I trust God with my heart. I gave my heart—such a precious commodity—to someone who could not and would not treasure it. Meanwhile, I knew that God wanted me to give it all over to Him. That was too precarious an offer for me to accept. Isn't that something? Have you ever continued to give yourself over to something that had proven itself detrimental to you rather than trust the unknown that comes with giving yourself over to God? I wouldn't even give God a chance. Although verbally and in my journals, I begged God to make a change, I actively resisted surrendering all that came in direct conflict with change being possible. I was too afraid to really trust God with my hopes and dreams.

The evening before Thanksgiving, we hung out at my house after service and I baked an extra pie for him to take to his aunt's house. Why? I was always the one to call him—the action was never reciprocated, and even when we did speak, the conversation was more about him, with no interest in my life. Then, the conversations began to take a turn with him sharing the woes with the ex-girlfriend he was still going back and forth with. But, to be fair, why wouldn't he share these things with me? Wasn't I just a friend? His good ol' sister in Christ? It was me who was putting more expectations and hope on this relationship than there was. I was allowing my feelings to keep me in a dead place.

Regardless of how wonderful my relationship with Greg had been, it was over and I just could not come to terms with it, cut my losses, and walk away. This was the same woman who was feeling unfulfilled in the relationship and asked God for guidance. God answered and instructed me to end it and I did. I had one moment of being brave and moving by faith and in obedience. But life is made up of a series of acts of faith and obedience—not just one. I disregarded all that God had told me that night by continuing to make myself available to Greg emotionally, by still pining after him. I wasn't surrendered to God. I only wanted God to give me my desired outcome. One that did not include heartbreak or challenges. Since I could not have that, I was trying to make my own pleasant outcome and I was using the same tired old tools that had always landed me in heartbreak hotel. If Greg had asked to get back together during this time, I would have done it without thinking twice—even though God had instructed me otherwise. That is not obedience at all. That is trying to manipulate God long enough to get your way. However, all of the charm, persuasion, and pleading did not work. Neither Greg nor God were budging. I could not have my way.

Let's add another layer to this by establishing that Greg had become quite the popular catch at church. I hate the stereotype that women flock to single men in the church, but there was definitely some flocking going on. Most people did not know that we had dated, so some women had even gone to my mother asking if her nephew Greg was single. My mom, always on my side and my ferocious protector, God bless her, would become indignant and make sure that the inquirer knew that it was I who had brought him to the church, and that we were not cousins but had dated seriously. This was, of course, in the hopes that the woman would immediately apologize and pray for my reconciliation with Greg. Ehhh, not so much.

Greg had increased his participation in the Usher Board and would now be at both services, much to my dismay. There was no getting away from him. It was quite a sight to see the gaggle of women surrounding him after service, inviting him to lunch, to their singles get-togethers at their home...to any and everything. Their persistent attempts served as a mirror held up before my face. Was I so different? Not really. But I wanted to be. I wanted to get over it. I was ready to. I stopped trying.

By the time Christmas came, our friendship had fizzled. I was now just a face to say hi to on a Sunday among the many. We would see each other at events like birthday parties and weddings of our church friends. He would be on one side of the room with his friends and I would be with my family. I did not really have too many friends yet and the ones I did have were his friends now too—so, yes, that was awkward. At some parties, a merengue or something would come on, everyone would be on the dance floor, and we'd end up dancing together, mostly because we were often among the few Latinos in the room and it's only fun when you are dancing with someone who knows what they are doing. We didn't talk when we danced, we just danced in an easy way, like people who knew what the next move would be. When the song was over, we'd nod and return to our corners without any dialogue. Once or twice after an event, I'd get a phone call with him telling me I looked nice and it was good to see me. They would be short, light conversations filled with jokes and niceties and was never followed up with anything else. We grew farther and farther part until I no longer knew what his day-to-day life was like. I didn't know where he worked or his latest favorite movie. We were no longer friends. It was really over.

I went to work and shared my heartbreak with my team who were truly now my friends. They prayed for and encouraged me. James asked, "You didn't kiss this guy, did you?" I pretended not to hear him and quickly changed the subject. I was able to have more frank conversations with other female friends at work. They understood the longing for a mate and also the real, relentless struggle of keeping the flesh in check. Someone suggested a book for single Christian women. It was called *Knight in Shining Armor*. The methodology of the book was to stop dating for six months and just focus on God. At the end of the six months, the author met her husband. Six months, huh? That seemed doable. So, I went through the six months diligently. I read the book, learned more about God, joined the choir, and gave no man the time of day. The six months actually felt pretty good because I was choosing not to date, so I felt more in control, like there was an amazing end in sight. I remember when the six months were ending, I was at the airport waiting to welcome in some prospective students who were flying in for a visit. What better place to be at than an airport to meet your future husband? There were thousands of people passing through; surely, we would bump into each other or he'd come over to me for directions and we'd instantly connect. It'd be the stuff from a Rom-Com but in real life. I applied another layer of lip gloss and tried to look aloof, mysterious and like a future wife. I probably looked good and crazy. Thousands of men passed by. My students arrived. My husband didn't.

Six months gave way to two years. Yes, you read that right. Once the six months were up, God impressed on me to take it further. To take a step back with putting effort into finding a mate and focus elsewhere. So, I did, and in the next chapter I will tell you what that actually ended up looking like. But at this point, it was two years later and it was Springtime again, a time when fleeting memories of that Springtime with Greg would creep up, even for a moment.

It was a Sunday, and the weather was absolutely gorgeous. Warm, slightly breezy and sunny. I had gone home with Kiera after service and was deciding how we would frolic that afternoon when my phone rang. It was Greg, the last person I had expected. I had not spoken to him in months.

"Days like this make me think about when we used to hang out," he said in that velvety voice. Up to this point, I had been okay. I had remained single and was focusing on my daughter and my career. I had started a new job at a nonprofit and gone back to school for a Master's Degree in Nonprofit Administration. I also was singing in the choir and growing closer to God. I was at peace. This was unexpected. My heart raced as he continued, "What are you doing today? Beatrice and I are going over to Jackson Hole Burgers on 86th Street. Do you and Kiera want to come?"

I wasn't sure what to make of it. I was excited but a little confused. But more excited for sure. "Okay," I replied, "We can meet you guys over there."

I was in a good enough place to keep my cool and pray on the walk over there. An old friend wanting to hang out in the most platonic manner with a mutual friend and my daughter in tow. I could do this, right? I asked God to make this crystal clear and to protect me. The afternoon was very enjoyable. We went to Jackson Hole and had burgers. Then we walked over to the ice cream shop for dessert. I remember him helping himself to a bite of my ice cream with the greatest of ease. Like, no concern for cooties at all. The way one would share with a friend. After ice cream, we walked to Best Buy where he and Beatrice bought the newly released iPod shuffles. These were the very first, you guys! The kind that came on a lanyard so you could wear them around your neck. They were so excited to finally own this cool new piece of technology. I laugh as I write this because many people reading this will not even know what I am talking about. Google it!

After walking around a bit more, laughing and joking, we walked uptown where they took the bus back to the West Side and Kiera and I walked the rest of the way home. I did not know what to think. This afternoon could not have gone any easier and been more pleasant, but something in me was stirred awake – that hope that we would be together again. Later that afternoon, I called Beatrice, who was friends with me, but even closer to Greg. She told me how she even noticed our rapport and asked him what was up on their bus ride home and he said that he had a lot of respect and love for me.

"Girl, there is a chance that we will never be together," I told her.

She replied "But there's a chance you will," then quickly followed it with "I've already said too much."

What did that mean? I tried to contain excitement. I remember writing in my journal later that day and asking God to make it all clear and give me closure once and for all. Either the last bits of feeling in me would be eradicated by the outcome of all of this or the dreams that I kept stuffed down deep in my heart would come true.

Kiera and I left for our annual Florida vacation a week later, and as I laid by the pool, I replayed that Sunday and became more convinced that all signs pointed to it being our time. My six months was just a bit extended but alas, this was it. I imagined us finally reuniting. Now that we had almost two years of pruning and growth under our belts, we could finally be together and do it God's way. I became elated at this thought. It made perfect sense. I purchased a little Florida license plate keychain that said "Greg" at a gift shop. I could hardly wait to get back to New York and present him with the little seemingly unassuming token to let him know that he had been on my mind. He would put it on his keys and think of me whenever he opened a door.

The next Sunday I was in church, I could hardly contain my excitement. I was freshly tanned and ready for my moment. All of the books on singleness and waiting had prepared me for this day. Sure, it had taken almost two years, but it was all worth it. That particular Sunday, Pastor Bobby, our choir director, was trying out a new formation for the choir where we would sit on the choir stand throughout service, facing the congregation. As I sat there, I caught a glimpse of my knight in shining armor in the balcony dutifully ushering congregants. I sang my heart out that day, so grateful to God for what He had done in my life.

When we sat back down, I looked up and saw Greg in the balcony, and I thought to myself how amazing he looked as an usher. *Look at him*, I thought to myself, *so strong and charming. I love that slightly bowlegged walk of his. He's so kind too, look at him guiding in that young woman. He's walking her all the way to the pew.* Then I was jolted out of my daydream as reality unfolded in front of me. If the pews had been pillows, he would have fluffed them for this mystery woman. Seeing this moment of "deluxe-level" ushering made me wonder, but maybe it was a coworker of his or something. Greg and I had both invited many friends to church over the past couple of years. Nothing to be concerned about.

Between services, a group of us would always go to the Key West Diner, on Broadway and 94th street, for breakfast. This was one of the fun parts of the day and we would get recharged for second service while the kids were in Sunday school—well, my kid at least. Most of my choir friends were single with no kids. I started chatting with one such friend who was sitting next to me. You know that person who is always in the know? That person who is consistently made privy to the tea in other people's lives? Yes, that's her. Although I try to stay away from gossip, I needed to find out if I was being silly in believing that what I saw during service meant something. So, I leaned into my source and inquired casually about who the woman at service was.

"Babyyyyy," began my dependable Know it All. "They went to so and so's party a couple of weeks ago and have been inseparable ever since." As the last word left Know it All's lips, I felt my hopes dashed and my dreams shatter into a million pieces. My heart sank into the pit of my stomach and I tried to hold back tears. We left the diner and as I walked down Broadway, back toward church, I tried with all of my might to break in half that stupid keychain that I had bought. When it wouldn't break, I tossed it into the trash. How could I have been so stupid? I had come so very far only to have an almost-completely-healed wound torn open.

That afternoon service was by far the hardest for me to get through. There I sat, in plain view of the entire congregation and trying to hold back my tears of hurt and disappointment.

After service, Greg saw me in the lobby and came over to me. "How are you?"

How am I? I thought. *You sack of hot manure... I let myself be open to you and you break my heart yet again.*

My response was some unrehearsed corny line about having learned that he is in a relationship and hoping that he is happy before I stormed away. Have you ever walked away from a conversation and thought, man I wish I had a better comeback than that? That mixed with the hurt of this news had me trying with all of my might not to ugly-cry right there in the church lobby. Just three or four years prior to this, I would have run to the store to get cigarettes and a bottle of Bacardi and numbed myself to deal with the pain. Now I just wanted to hear from someone who knew God. Someone who could pour the living water of God's Word on my wound. As I went toward the back of the church, I thankfully saw Pastor Bobby and made a beeline toward him.

"Can we talk?" I asked as my voice quivered. He looked at me with a fleeting expression of surprise at seeing me so upset, which was quickly followed by a warm smile. "Sure, let's go to my office," he replied.

We walked up the three flights to his office, which gave me a chance to compose myself. He sat behind his desk and I sat on the edge of the couch, not even knowing how to begin to speak.

"What happened?" Pastor Bobby asked.

"My heart is broken," I replied, my voice quivering once again. I then went on to explain that while I foolishly thought that Greg and I would be reconciling, I found out that he had started seeing someone else.

"Wait, so you and Greg dated before? Oh yeah I forgot that you brought him to this church," he said.

Wow, so there was really not even a memory that he and I had ever been. Of course, there wasn't—it was years ago. There was what seemed like a lifetime of new memories and friendships that had happened between then and the night that God told me to break it off. Did I even have a right to be upset at this point? Did I bring this all on myself? At this, I started weeping again.

"You know that God sees every one of these tears and is collecting them," Pastor Bobby continued in his chipper and encouraging way.

"But what do I do now?" I pleaded.

"You pray for them, for the both of them. You don't know what God is doing and they need prayer."

This was not what I wanted to hear. Not at all. How could I pray for two people whom I really could not stand at that moment? How could I ask for God to bless Greg without me being part of that blessing? This was beyond me. The one thing I knew for sure was that I had to let go. I had to find the resolve within me to relinquish the hope of a future for me and Greg in exchange for the future that God had for me. I went home that day and as soon as Kiera and I walked in the house, I ran to the bathroom,

> Rejection shook every piece of truth about my worth that I had been gleaning from God. It exposed every insecurity I was trying so hard to overcome. I allowed it to taunt me; I repeated its taunts to myself and believed them.

closed the door, and wept on the floor. Then I cleaned my face and went on with being a mom, trying not to let on that I was heartbroken.

The next weeks were similar. I would see them together, hold in the hurt, rush home after service and cry out to God on my bathroom floor. I felt like such a loser. Greg's new girlfriend was beautiful, fashionable, sweet, and she was not a single mom.

As a single mom, there is often that thought that men, especially those who are unattached, would not seriously consider us. We are marred in some way and not preferable at all. So to me, here was this woman who was everything that I was not. He fawned over her in front of everyone. They would hold hands and wear matching designer blazers with jeans and were just one of the cutest couples I had ever seen. This cut me deeply, not just because they were together, but because it felt like this rejection confirmed what I had suspected...Greg was presented with the option of getting back together with me or this new exciting woman who was unattached. He had not chosen me. On top of that, all our mutual friends had seen this play out. They knew that I had been the loser. I was not worthy. No one would want to seriously love a single mom unless they were a parent themselves, or a jerk, or weirdo. I was only good for flings and fun, but when it came down to commitment, I would never be chosen. I began to lose hope that I would ever find healthy love.

Rejection shook every piece of truth about my worth that I had been gleaning from God. It exposed every insecurity I was trying so hard to overcome. I allowed it to taunt me; I repeated its taunts to myself and believed them. The thoughts that manifested as a result of rejection pulled mercilessly at my sense of hope, as if in some spiritual tug of war where I was the lone weakling. The truth is that not everyone you desire will desire you in return, even if you have it ALL going on. "To each his own," as my mom often said. But my goodness, it's not that easy to accept this truth sometimes, especially when you are so committed to the idea of being with a person. My friend, it hurts, but we cannot allow ourselves to stay in those places. How do we deal with rejection and the thoughts and feelings that haunt us because of disappointment?

I know God was with me, but real talk, I struggled. I was having consistent bawling sessions on my bathroom floor, for goodness sake. But between those sessions, I kept on going. I kept breathing, even though sometimes it would hurt to breathe. Isn't it amazing how we can sometimes physically feel a broken heart? Hurting or not, I mothered my Kiki, I went to work by day and grad school by night, I kept taking care of myself even though on many days, I doubted my beauty and worth. I journaled...so...much. I asked God to do the work to heal me, knowing I couldn't handle it myself. When it was nighttime, prime-time for feeling restless, lonely and hopeless, I read, wrote and repeated Bible verses that became absolute lifelines for me. I repeated the lines until I fell asleep. I recited them when I was on the subway and jolted with sadness. I declared them when I was tired of the negative thoughts trying to pull me into a muddy pit of despair. I did not want to think or feel that way anymore. I wanted to fight back. These scriptures were my weapon.

The Lord is close to the broken hearted and saves those who are crushed in spirit. (Psalm 34:18)

Regardless of who may have wanted nothing to do with me, the Lord was close to me. He was holding me, and even though I was crushed, I was still safe with Him.

The Lord is my light and my salvation —
whom shall I fear? The Lord is the stronghold of my

life —
of whom shall I be afraid? (Psalm 27:1)

While I was not afraid of anyone outwardly, my thoughts haunted me. I was afraid of what my future held. I feared what people thought of me. But God is my light and my salvation; all of those factors are inconsequential. Who in and out of the world is greater than God? I had nothing to fear.

When the wicked advance against me
to devour me,
it is my enemies and my foes
who will stumble and fall.
Though an army besiege me,
my heart will not fear;
though war break out against me,
even then I will be confident. (Psalm 27:2-3)

I was under regular attack by my thoughts, and it seemed like I would never win. The enemy was poised to destroy me starting with my mind. There was an advance against me, and it wanted to undo everything that God had done thus far and render me hopeless and useless. But the joke was on the enemy. In spite of being in battle, I could rest assured that I would win, even if I did not feel like I was.

One thing I ask from the Lord,
this only do I seek:
that I may dwell in the house of the Lord
all the days of my life,
to gaze on the beauty of the Lord
and to seek him in his temple. (Psalm 27:4)

Oh my goodness, this is one of my favorite passages of scripture of all time, and it's a continual desire! I want this, more than anything; more than anyone. I want to dwell with God! Being in His presence and taking in His beauty outshines the best day that I could ever have with anyone else.

For in the day of trouble
he will keep me safe in his dwelling;
he will hide me in the shelter of his sacred tent
and set me high upon a rock. (Psalm 27:5)

When I am hurt, it's hard to feel safe. Vulnerability can leave me feeling exposed and unsure. There is a place where I find refuge and can be completely myself, leaving my wounds exposed to be tended to without judgment or ulterior motive. That place is in God.

Then my head will be exalted
above the enemies who surround me;

at his sacred tent I will sacrifice with shouts of joy;
I will sing and make music to the Lord. (Psalm 27:6)

Since I know whose I am and my bowed head will be exalted by my God, I can get really confident about it and celebrate! I don't need to know how it will all work out; I choose to worship God and be joyful now!

Hear my voice when I call, Lord;
be merciful to me and answer me.
My heart says of you, "Seek his face!"
Your face, Lord, I will seek.
Do not hide your face from me,
do not turn your servant away in anger;
you have been my helper.
Do not reject me or forsake me,
God my Savior.
Though my father and mother forsake me,
the Lord will receive me. (Psalm 27:7-10)

And when I began to question whether God was listening to me, when the toxic lie that what I had done in life prevented me from receiving grace, mercy and favor, I honestly had to bring those thoughts to Him. I also had to keep reminding myself, like David did, to "Seek His face!"

Teach me your way, Lord;
lead me in a straight path
because of my oppressors.
Do not turn me over to the desire of my foes,
for false witnesses rise up against me,
spouting malicious accusations. (Psalm 27:11-12)

I wanted to learn from my trials. I didn't want to handle things in a way that was contrary to God's character and will. My prayer was, "People will talk and people will think, but please, God, do not let me bow under the pressure of the whims and opinions of people."

I remain confident of this:
I will see the goodness of the Lord
in the land of the living. (Psalm 27:13)

This is where faith came in. I had no idea what was to come in my life. I had no idea if God would answer my prayers the way I wanted or if He would take another course altogether. Regardless, I had to believe that whatever He allowed in my life would be good, was for my good and that I would rejoice again.

Wait for the Lord;
be strong and take heart

and wait for the Lord. (Psalm 27:14)

This was the verse that I constantly had on REPEAT in my heart and mind both as an encouragement and a directive:

> *Be strong and take heart* – Lydia, you have not lost. You are not a loser. Don't act like the loser.
>
> *Be strong and take heart* – Lydia, you can smile again. You have reason to be joyful right where you are.
>
> *Be strong and take heart* – Lydia, don't let this take you down girl, get up and out and keep living.
>
> *Be strong and take heart* – Lydia, do not succumb to the pull of revenge or bitterness, trust God with it all.
>
> *Be strong and take heart* – Lydia, do not close yourself off. There is love around you in many forms. Give and receive freely.
>
> *Wait on the Lord* – Lydia, put that phone down! Do not send that email! Leave it in God's hands.
>
> *Wait on the Lord* – Lydia, you are God's now, be pure and be His bride in waiting.
>
> *Wait on the Lord* – Lydia, let go of the old way of comforting yourself and stay in His presence.
>
> *Wait on the Lord* – *Lydia,* stick to God like your life depends on it! Let Him into every area and consider Him in all things.

There was no way I could spend that much time redirecting my mind and meditating on the Word of God and not begin to experience victory. Victory was not getting completely over it in a flash, but being just fine. Victory was burrowing myself deeper under the shadow of God's wings. Victory was showing up for life and not using my hurt as a crutch to prevent me from showing up for my responsibilities. Victory was slowly pulling on that rope of hope and not letting go. Victory is growing through pain. Our choir was learning a new song and I was asked to sing the solo part. The song was called "Changed" by Tremaine Hawkins. It's a song about a life that is changed but not perfect. A life that has been redeemed and is determined not to go back. A life that now wants to serve God. My life.

I was asked to sing this song at the Amsterdam Avenue festival where our choir had a bandstand. We faced south toward the entire festival and could see down for blocks and blocks. I had prayed for God to make things clear. I had prayed to be used by God and get out of my own way. I had prayed to get closer to God and know His love for me. I began to sing "Changed" when I saw, right in front of me, Greg and his girlfriend, holding hands and walking off together to enjoy the festival. I closed my eyes and kept singing. Everything was made painfully clear. But, instead of feeling dread, I felt relieved for the clarity, and so very loved by God. The rejection was not an indictment on me. The rejection was part of God's protection and plan. I would wait, be strong, take heart, and wait for the Lord.

FOOD *for* THOUGHT

"My child, pay attention to what I say. Listen carefully to my words. Don't lose sight of them. Let them penetrate deep into your heart, for they bring life to those who find them, and healing to their whole body." (Proverbs 4:20–22 NLT)

- Are you bitter about a past relationship? Are you harboring feelings of resentment? Has it been difficult for you to get over it? How about praying for that person who hurt you? Not in a "Dear Lord, get 'em!" kind of way, but honestly praying for their well-being and relationship with the Lord.

- The word of God is light and life. It is what we need at all times, but especially in our darkest moments. What scriptures can you meditate on as you journey towards healing your broken heart?

CHAPTER *Six*

THE JESUS DIET

Recently, I was in a meeting with a group of colleagues, most of whom were also mental health professionals. One woman talked about a model being used to help people with addictions move toward sustained, healthy, independent lives. She mentioned the Theory of Change, a concept created by James Prochasta and Carlo DiClemente in the late 1970s to address those trying to quit smoking.[1]

What does this have to do with anything that you and I are talking about? So much, so stay with me! There are six stages in the Theory of Change and I realized, as I listened to my colleague talk, that they resonated with me a lot.

According to the first theory, the first stage is precontemplation. That's the stage when you do not even think that you have a problem. The activities that you choose to engage in are not seen as having any negative effects on your life and you are not interested in even considering change. This was me when I first started attending church begrudgingly and hiding in the balcony. I was just fine with my life the way it was. My toxic relationships and behaviors were something temporary I thought would be a means to the end

I wanted. There was absolutely nothing wrong with being "sexual-ly free", regularly drinking hard alcohol to induce sleep and chain smoking as a means of relaxation and coping, and no one could convince me otherwise. Even though I was hiding these behaviors from most people, it wasn't because I thought it was wrong. It was because I didn't want to be judged. Especially by some judgmental, prudish religious person. People in the precontemplation stage are not trying to hear anyone's advice or admonishment, so the best one can do at this point is pray for them. Which my mom and her gang of prayer warriors did!

The next stage is contemplation. Contemplation is when you recognize that there could be some benefits to changing certain be-haviors, but you believe that what you would have to give up far outweighs what you would get in return. This was me when I at-tended church regularly and enjoyed the music and messages, but left and immediately returned to business as usual. I was saved and loved how God made me feel. I heard testimonies of how other people who pursued God seemed to have peace and even blessings and I wanted that. I simply could not reconcile how I could ever be happy without the behaviors I had become accustomed to. I was also afraid that giving these behaviors up and trusting God to run things would be so boring and corny. The contemplation stage is described as being heavy in ambivalence toward the behaviors that need to change. Ambivalence is defined as contradictory ideas or mixed feelings about something.[2] Basically, we run hot and cold for God, dipping our toes in and out of the water. During this stage I would cry out to God to help me, but I wouldn't dare do anything on my part to ensure that change occur.

Next comes preparation, which is also called determination. In this stage, you start gathering information, doing research and making plans to change. You may even make small changes during this stage. For me, I know this largely occurred during my season at The King's College. God plucked me out of the kind of workplace I was used to and I was immersed in an environment where I could ask questions, see faith in action, and begin to believe that change could be for me too. I often think back to when I told Greg about my two-month rule and how ludicrous and non-biblical it was. But, it also was change. A few months before that, I would not have even considered how God felt about my personal choices. Yes, I was still in sin but I had a desire to choose God. That's progress and it was the best I knew to do at that time. Besides, God wasn't finished with me. I was reading His Word, developing my relationship with Him through worship and quiet time, which resulted in a more resolute change in my thinking just a few months later.

Research shows that people who skip this stage of preparation and go straight to the next are more likely to relapse within fifteen days. At first glance, it seems easier to just stop doing something out of will power, but studies show it will not last. I could have just stopped doing what I was doing, but without a core understanding and belief in my "Why"; without a true desire to make the change and trust that it would indeed lead me to the life I wanted, then I would just go back to my old ways. Following rules without a heart change is religion. It is like living by the law as the Israelites did before Jesus came on the scene. I really did not want religion. I still don't. Looking perfect on the outside wasn't what I saw in others that resonated with me. It was their relationship with God. The confidence they had because they knew who they belonged to. The peace and grace they walked in that allowed them to be infectiously joyful, that's what resonated with me. I wanted God and because I wanted God, I wanted to please Him. The preparation stage was my heart-changing stage and it was where I became truly invested in wanting to change.

> *Following rules without a heart change is religion. It is like living by the law as the Israelites did before Jesus came on the scene. I really did not want religion. I still don't.*

The next stage of change is action, and we are going to park here for a little while. Action is just what it says. It is when intentions become movement. It's when everything that has been inside of you, largely unbeknownst to others, becomes evident as you begin to do things in a new way. The evidence of your private time seeking God is lived out in public. Even with all the determination in the world, this action stage does not just happen effortlessly. I look back at my journals from 2003 to 2005, and although I find myself engaged in heavy eye-rolling and sighing while reading page after page about my pathetic, undying devotion to someone who did not return the sentiment, I also saw how much I poured out everything openly before God. Self-centered prayers morphed to God-centered prayers. I slowly went from, "God, give me the desires of my heart—a man, strong finances, a promotion at work" to "God, help me be in love with you, show me your will for my life, use me in the lives of others so that they can know you too". My language changed; my dependence on myself and my own bright ideas and capabilities was replaced with imploring God to get into every aspect of my life no matter how big or small. I was different. Not perfect, but changing, day by day. Of course, I still struggled. I had moments of loneliness and weakness. I called ex-boyfriends—like busted and disgusted exes just because I wanted to feel wanted. But even that eventually fell away. Like the song I sang, something began to change in me. The relationship with God I always thought was for other people, those seemingly perfect people, now began to blossom in me. I loved God, and instead of a battle between His will and my own, it was me wanting His ways to become my own.

I have been on a diet or two (or ten) in my life, whether in preparation for a beach vacation, or trying to shed that additional winter insulation that accumulated via hibernation and intense consumption of comfort food and snacks. The dictionary defines a diet as restricting oneself to small amounts or special kinds of food to lose weight.[3] I had so much weight I was carrying around that I desperately wanted to lose. I am not referring to physical weight, but the emotional and spiritual baggage that had held me back for so long. I wanted to lose that broken heart, lose my need for affirmation from men to make me feel worthy, lose lust, and lose my twisted perspective about what it meant to be successful and leave a mark on the world. Anyone who knows about good nutrition knows that it is not enough just to stop eating junk. You also have to introduce healthy foods into the mix. I wanted to be in position to regularly feast on spiritual nutrition, like accepting that I was deeply loved by God and allowing that Truth to heal me. I wanted to feast on the Truth about my position as a child of God and letting that be enough. I wanted to delve into and understand His word enough to wield it against every attack. I wanted to understand my God-given purpose and be courageous enough to run after that and not fleeting worldly success. But most of all, I wanted contentment and peace.

One thing about me is that I am really good at procrastinating, reasoning myself out of things I am really not into, and going halfway when my heart is not in it. However, when I really decide to do something, I go all in. There is a go-getter in me that I wish would come out more often, but she really shows up when it counts. God did not force me to make changes in my life; I wanted to. It was my decision to get out of the lukewarm, stagnant pool I had been wading aimlessly in, and plunge into the deep waters of intimacy with God that would lead to a new focused chapter of my life. Hey, if you want something different, you've got to start doing things differently. I was not just singing about a change happening, and I wasn't just asking God to change me without any participation on my part. I had to do my part. As I write this, I'm thinking about a song I absolutely LOVE by Jonathan McReynolds called "Make Room". Please listen to it when you have a chance. The song is about making room for God. It speaks about moving things (our schedule, plans, egos, attitudes, etc.) out the way so that God can dwell with us. That's where I was, I wanted to move things out the way to make room for God. God and I were in it together. There were areas where I saw a need for adjustments and made them. There were areas that led to me feeling more trepidation, and so God allowed situations to occur where I had to choose Him over those things. Not sure what I mean? Well, here are some ways this all played out:

How I Spent My Time

There was a time when a weekend could not pass by without me going out and partying; but, I'll take it that you've already gathered that. What was a weekend without partying? After a while though, I just had no desire to go out anymore. Now, I am not saying there is anything wrong with going out and enjoying yourself. Truth be told, nowadays I love it when I get an opportunity for a night out with friends or with my husband. The love of salsa dancing has never left me, and I also recently discovered that I'm really into singing show-tunes at Karaoke! So, it's not the going out and having fun that is wrong...it was the need to be out. It was the search for fulfillment and affirmation that I thought could be satiated by dressing up and being ogled and propositioned by complete strangers. It was being on a tight income, yet easily spending $60 or more (nothing to sneeze at for a single mom in the early 2000's) on cover charges and drinks in the hopes that something amazing would come out of the night. It never did.

So, where I removed some things, I also replaced some things.

Friday night parties were replaced with family night. I would order take-out and Kiera and I would cuddle on the couch and watch movies. Once she fell asleep, I'd turn on Turner Classics and get lost in an old movie. My supervisor at my new job knew how to knit, and I remembered how to crochet from my mom. We taught each other these skills and so some nights I would have such a peaceful time making handcrafted items and watching movies or listening to music. I also started attending Bible study, as well as small groups plus I began taking grad school classes two nights a week. On Saturdays, it was off to take Kiera to her ballet classes and sometimes have lunch with a friend, or we'd go on outings to the museum, bookstore, or do crafts at home. I found that my hobbies brought me such enjoyment, and as corny as that sounds, crafting and DIY still remains a significant part of my life. I find it therapeutic. Between classes, choir rehearsal, and enjoying my family, my time was so full that I didn't even want to add anything else to my schedule. I didn't even miss the club—at all.

What I Fed My Mind

Romans 12:2 advises us not to be conformed to the pattern of this world, but be transformed by the renewing of our minds. It's not enough for us to will certain thoughts and mindsets away, we have to replace them with the Truth. This does not mean that we just listen to the Bible twenty-four hours a day, although if you can, go for it! I found that certain music, movies and books were triggers for me. I mean, listen to an entire Isley Brothers album followed by

Maxwell and then some 90's R&B, and you are bound to get into a frisky state of mind. I used to listen to this music all the time. I mean, these artists are amazing, but if I wanted to get free from lustful thoughts and lamenting over wanting to be with someone, I had to put these albums away for a while. Through being in the choir, I became familiar with Christian artists and added them to my rotation. Music has such power. I would find myself encouraged, uplifted and sustained after listening to gospel albums while I cleaned, drove around running errands, or just relaxed at home. Truth and scripture-focused lyrics were wafting through my home's atmosphere, and it made such a difference.

I also had to put a pause on binging on movies with graphic sex scenes. Before you look at me sideways and tell me I am doing too much right now, hear me out. I had decided that I was no longer going to be sexually active until I was married—like, for real. The reality is, all of our actions begin with thoughts. Sometimes, the thoughts are fleeting and we cast them down. Sometimes, we let our guard down and entertain them for a little while, either to pass the time or escape into some pseudo form of comfort. Since an entry into our mind has been left open, the thoughts may come back a little while later, or even the next day. Because they seem harmless, we let them back in. They play a little longer. We let them. The next time, they come back sooner than they did before. The thoughts become acceptable to us because they are harmless, they are just in our heads, and frankly they make us feel good. We now call them to mind pretty often. Then, because we have an enemy who wants to take us down in a billowy pyre of sin and shame, an opportunity to engage in something regarding that thought that we have normalized comes up. Because we have already played this out in our minds, it is easier for our bodies to follow the lead. At best, we sin, feel awful, repent and turn away. At worst, we do something that we never intended and can never take back—something that causes harm to self and others in the process. So yes, I had to fast forward through some scenes in movies and avoid others altogether because I was on a mission to finally be free from lust and I would be darned if a steamy scene from a movie was going to trip me up.

People I Surrounded Myself With

I have always been blessed with such amazing friends and, saved or not, they all pretty much had their acts together while I was the hot mess of the group. It started with Selina, whom I met in middle school and grew close to when I was bullied out of the group of friends I had. That was one of the best things to ever happen to me. Over the years, we collected more amazing friends in high school and up to college, where she and I pledged two different sororities and managed to widen our circles. Selina, Kiera and I lived in the apartment on the fifth floor of the building where I grew up, and we had a blast. My friends stood by me when I drunk-called guys and let me cry on them when I was heartbroken yet again. We celebrated and cried together. We had countless girls' nights and game nights at our place and laughed late into the night. They have always been fun, kind and fiercely loyal.

In addition to the friends I already enjoyed, God allowed my circle to be broadened yet again with friends from church. I don't even remember how I met Wendy, but I do remember that she did our hair and makeup for our singing group's photo shoots and somehow, we developed a rapport. Wendy was younger than I was and married to her high school sweetheart with two kids. Not only was Wendy so immensely kind and gracious, but she also absolutely adored Jesus and was unapologetic about it. I met Josette when I started singing in church. Josette has one of the most amazing voices I have ever heard. She and I didn't exactly hit it off immediately because I was so intimidated by her depth of scriptural knowledge and maturity in God, but when we finally did hang out, we realized how much we have in common and have been close ever since. We also were both single at the time, which helped me not to feel alone. Josette, Wendy and I started hanging out, mostly at Wendy's house. Kiera would play with Wendy's kids and the three of us would talk, do hair and pray—a lot. When we weren't hanging out, we were on the phone talking and praying—a lot. Wendy's husband, Junior, started calling us the Holy Homegirls. I do not know how I would have fared without these women. Although they were both young women, they had already had long walks of faith with the Lord and had such wisdom and life experiences to share with me. We were all candid with each other and held each other accountable with our particular struggles. When one of us was struggling with hope, we spoke God's Word and encouragement into her. We went to battle for one another in the spirit.

I also had other friends and acquaintances, many of which I partied my hardest with. These friendships eventually changed. After taking a pass on outing after outing, they stopped inviting me out. One friend told me over the phone that I had changed, I wasn't fun anymore. She said she wanted the old Lydia back. Now let me say that if God had given me a glimpse of this conversation before I ran to the altar and gave my life to Jesus, I probably wouldn't have moved out of the pew. I probably would have been dissuaded by the thought of friends telling me that I was no longer any fun. However, at that time, I honestly could not care less. I had a new concept of fun in my life and no one could convince me that I was not in a much better place than I was before. I may not have been getting anymore invitations to go out, I may not have had as many friends as I once did, but I did have a core group of ride-or-dies who were helping me to flourish. I had my share of friends who gave practical advice, but I needed biblical truth. I had my share of friends who would go late into the night with me in drinking and debauchery, but I needed friends who would pray and fast into the night with me. I had my share of friends who wanted to amass clothes, bags, shoes and be rich and famous, but I needed friends who wanted to amass treasures in heaven. Yes, God allowed some friendships to dissipate, but it was for my good.

My Goals and Dreams

On top of grad school and my other hobbies, I had also been in a singing group since I graduated from college. Soul Tres was our name and it was comprised of Selina, Tracy—our friend from college, and me. Interestingly, Pastor Bobby, who I am pretty sure was not even a pastor yet but led the choir, would arrange our music. Our music was a pop/R&B style, and he, with this background in music (he studied in conservatory) and God-given talent, would create beautiful harmonies for us. I had dreams of making it one day and being a music sensation. There are countless pages in my journals where I prayed for a record deal, talked about the latest showcase where we sang, and even tried my hand at writing lyrics (which I can say is NOT my gifting). Although we started singing together in 2000, recorded songs in the studio with our own money and even had a full-length concert at the local cultural center, complete with costume changes and choreography, we were nowhere near our big break.

My godbrother, Leroy, started Soul Tres because I suspect he saw star potential in me. Leroy always had me performing in musicals as a kid. He created East Harlem urban versions of well-known musicals like *Cats* and even *The Wizard of Oz* and would find a role for me every time, even as Evil Dorothy in the Wiz Part 2. Leroy had quite an imagination! Leroy also had me in a girl group when I was 11 or 12. We performed at block parties and even had our own rapper and back-up dancers. I loved singing and acting so there was absolutely no push-back on my end. With Leroy as our manager, Pastor Bobby arranging gorgeous melodies to our lyrics, and all of the time and money we invested in studio sessions, voice lessons and photo shoots, I believed we would be the next big thing. I could just see it. Kiera and I would be set for life. She'd have tutors because she'd be touring with me all over the world. I'd have to keep all of my rich and famous suitors at bay. I would cross over into film and Broadway and be an amazing triple threat artist. I would be the success I always dreamed of as a little girl. But, then I started having a conundrum.

I began to think, *I'm really not into the programs on MTV and BET. I don't even want to watch those channels, so…why was I striving to be on it one day?* There were these little changes in my attitude and thoughts toward certain things. Things that had never ever bothered me before, now mattered. I buried these feelings for the most part because I was already years into this and I did not want to be the one to quit. So, the year prior, I had joined the church choir. The annual choir retreat was in the summer of 2004 and I decided I'd give it a try. I had never been on a Christian retreat before and frankly, I was hoping this weekend away would result in major healing for my still sore heart.

Anyhow, here I was at the retreat and getting to know my fellow choir members. I really enjoyed the sessions as the facilitators were very down to earth and each spoke to where I was in my life. After a session on Day 2, Pastor Bobby asked us all to go and have complete quiet time with the Lord. This was new to me. I knew how to pray, read the Bible and journal out my thoughts until my fingers were stiff but sitting in utter silence, waiting for God to speak to me, well that was new and pretty intimidating. I found a quiet spot on the retreat center grounds and at first, I just sat and wrote to God. I started off writing about my heartbreak—it had probably been like 12 hours since the last time I came to Him with it and, you know, I wanted to keep it at the forefront of His mind. Then at some point, I just stopped because even though I wasn't making audible noise, I certainly was not being quiet before God. I stopped writing and just sat there, tried to clear my mind and waited. Then, I felt God speak to me—not like a voice from the outside, or like Jesus came and sat down next to me on the bench, but a phrase within me that felt too right to ignore. It was not what I was expecting to hear, but I wrote it down.

After quiet time, we all met up again in the conference room and Pastor Bobby asked if anyone wanted to share what they experienced. The room went silent. Most folks tried to keep their gaze down lest they were

> ...We were young unsaved women meeting with a single man, and there were plenty of people who were devout Christians who would have loved to have some free musical guidance from him. I could just imagine the religious pearls being clutched by people, thinking we were leading this poor man astray.

called on. It was one of those moments like the time I ran up to the altar. I felt like God was leaving the floor open just for me. The only thing was, I knew that once I uttered what He had spoken into my spirit, it would make it real. I would have to move on it. Almost unbeknownst by me, my hand began to rise. I can't tell you what I said entirely because I don't remember, and I am pretty sure I was crying and not completely coherent. I do, however remember finishing my statement by saying that God told me to leave my singing group and sing for His glory.

Pastor Bobby was visibly trying to contain his shock and then delight—because he loves when God takes people and turns their world upside down. I think the shock may have been more that he was also getting confirmation from the Lord— all of his hours spent with Soul Tres working on seemingly worldly endeavors was not in vain. Before I ever knew Pastor Bobby as a spiritual guide; way before I came to his office devastated about Greg, and before I ever would have considered joining a choir, Pastor Bobby had sat with Selina, Tracy and me in his office. He had prayed for us, encouraged us and loved us so nonjudgmentally that we were unsuspectingly but so openly receiving a glimpse into what God's love was like. Real talk, not everyone was supportive of him choosing to invest so heavily in us. We were not members of the church (I attended sporadically when we first began meeting with him), we were young unsaved women meeting with a single man, and there were plenty of people who were devout Christians who would have loved to have some free musical guidance from him. I could just imagine the religious pearls being clutched by people, thinking we were leading this poor man astray. But, unmoved by people and only by what the Holy Spirit put on his heart, Pastor Bobby, who wasn't a pastor at the time, kept meeting with Soul Tres. He kept encouraging us and praying for us and, after years of rehearsals and meetings, right at that choir retreat, God revealed one of the reasons why it had to be so.

It's one thing to get a clear Word from God and know exactly what you need to do; it's an entirely different thing to actually do it. The hard part of all of this would be telling my group mates, one of which was also my roommate, and both of which were dear friends, that I would be leaving the group. I was gagging as I thought about how I would tell them. We had so much invested, we had goals, and now I was walking away from all of that because God told me to. I deduced that I had better move on what God said and move quickly lest I lose my nerve.

That Sunday night after I returned from the retreat, I remember sitting at the kitchen table with Selina and with so much trepidation telling her what God had placed in my heart. I knew it was not what she was expecting to hear, and she had every right to be mad, disappointed and offended. But, in His most gracious and faithful way, God allowed Selina to take the news much better than I had expected. She told me she understood, that she had noticed a shift in me and it seemed for the better. Although it was a bit of a disappointment for her, she assured me that we were friends and I should never feel as if I could not come to her with something. I'm telling you guys, you don't need a lot of friends, just a core who really count, and this friend did and still does today. More importantly, do not be afraid to move in obedience to God and leave the consequences to Him. The three of us met with Pastor Bobby so that we could tell our third member, Tracy, and make sure that we would all be okay. We were all more than okay. Some relationships are not made strong until they go through some challenges, and this challenge certainly strengthened us. Selina and Tracy would continue to pursue music and even continued to meet with Pastor Bobby and rehearsed at our apartment. As for me, God had something else up his sleeve.

I was really enjoying singing in the choir and was content to use my voice in this manner for the rest of my life. I also enjoyed going to the annual Bobby Lewis Ensemble concert. The Ensemble, as you can gather from the name, was started by Pastor Bobby and included some of the most powerful and amazingly talented voices I had ever heard. Not only were these professional-level singers, but they were so incredibly anointed. The best of the best as far as I was concerned. It did not matter whether or not you were into gospel music, if you attended an Ensemble concert, you would undoubtedly be flabbergasted by the mix of rich velvety, sweet, powerhouse voices and moved to tears by the spirit that dwelled in every note sung. I was a fan. I knew their songs; I bought the CDs and sang out loud at home to my heart's content. I would invite my cousins, co-workers and even my neighbors to the Ensemble concert. If they were going to be singing at an event, I was there!

One Tuesday evening, after choir rehearsal at church, Serge, who assisted Pastor Bobby, told me he needed to speak with me. We sat in an unoccupied pew and it was a good thing I was sitting.

"Pastor Bobby would like for you to be the newest member of the Ensemble," he said, and then he searched my face, waiting in bated anticipation for my reaction. It took a second or two for the statement to register.

"Me, are you sure?" I asked, truly bewildered by how a pretty good—but not at all great—singer who, just a year before, had been singing "Gimme, gimme what I want and I'll give you, give you all of me" at a showcase, would be wanted in the Bobby Lewis Ensemble. I could not compare to these people, not by vocal ability or by spiritual depth.

Serge understood my concerns and assured me, "People ask to join the Ensemble all the time, but that's not how it works. Pastor Bobby prays and people are put on his heart, so it has less to do with raw talent and more to do with what God wants. You'll be fine." I guess I couldn't argue with that. Thus began one of the most fun and rewarding adventures of my life.

All of this transformation in my life was really a surrender. As I gave over to God something that at one point, I thought I would not be able to live without, He took it and returned something to me that was beyond my imagination. I never thought that I would be serving God. All of the things that I had been so afraid of trying because they were not fun enough ended up being so fulfilling.

Now, real talk, there are times, many times, when I have gone in so hard on a diet with the end goal of being fit, svelte and feeling good. I would stick to saying no to processed foods and carbs and I would work out until my legs shook and I wanted to throw up. I would stay the course for weeks and months and then, one day I would catch a glimpse of myself in the mirror and think to myself, "I have arrived, get it girl!" Then, I would forget that it's not enough to get to a healthy place, but to keep engaging in the same disciplines in order to stay there. I would slowly and steadily start incorporating sugary snacks, go for seconds because the food tasted good—not because I was hungry anymore, show up for my workouts, but cut corners when the burn intensified, and I'd find myself back where I was before, in even faster time than it took to get out.

It's the same with our walk. We may have seasons, often early on, where we are absolutely famished for God and seeking Him with reckless abandon. We are at every Bible study, we overhaul all that is not beneficial to us, we share the gospel with everyone who will listen and even those who don't want to. We are in deep. We experience deliverance and unprecedented love. We are healed, we are hopeful, and we are strong in Him. Then we take a look at ourselves. We realize that we have been changed and we like it, but we think the hard work is over. We breeze through prayer, skip small group meetings because we rationalize that we need a break. We change the radio station and leave it there—and the weight finds its way back into our souls.

I'm saying all of this with so much love and concern for you and me. Yes, most of this chapter has been about God changing me, and yes, I have been changed. But if for one minute I begin to think that I have arrived and there is nothing else to give over to God—if I begin to diminish the importance of the disciplines that I held fast to in order to thrive, if I am foolish enough to think that somehow I have an inner strength and will power apart from God that will ensure that I maintain where I have been brought to, then I have missed the point of it all. Diets don't work. They are a short-term solution that just cannot provide lasting results. If we want meaningful change, we need to change our lifestyle for good.

FOOD *for* THOUGHT

"Do not conform to the pattern of this world, but be transformed by the renewing of your mind. Then you will be able to test and approve what God's will is—his good, pleasing and perfect will." (Romans 12:2 NIV)

- Do you feel that God is shifting you from the familiar?
- Have you gotten comfortable? Have you been living a compromised life? How can you get back on track and refocus on Him? What steps can you take to reconnect and refocus?

CHAPTER Seven

PRACTICALLY 27 DRESSES

I knew beyond a shadow of a doubt that I was going to wait until marriage to be intimate with a man. I knew that I was forgiven and delivered from my past. I knew that God loved me, and I loved Him too. In 2005, I was turning twenty-eight years old and I wanted nothing more than to celebrate my birthday with Jesus and all of my family, friends and co-workers. So that's what I did. I rented out a performance space and all of my amazingly talented friends sang. Ensemble members, choir members and even my sweet Selina and Tracy all serenaded me. The place was packed with my parents, Kiera, siblings, cousins, friends, church friends, colleagues from my new job—it was amazing and it felt like all of the areas of my life were able to beautifully harmonize as though orchestrated by God Himself. It felt like a pivotal year for me, like I was celebrating the culmination of some really deep work that God had done in me, and now I was celebrating a new year of life and entering a season as a truly new creature in Christ.

I was so open about sharing the love of God with others. At work, at grad school, with the rest of my family and friends—everyone was introduced to Jesus. The one who was a hot mess was now the one that people were calling for prayer and guidance. Only God! I was being mentored by one of the most amazing women of God I have ever known, Minister Cheryl Wilson, who was on staff at my church. Minister Cheryl was also single and had been for a very long time. But she loved herself some Jesus and knew exactly how to both encourage and admonish me in love. Minister Cheryl began giving me assignments like praying over requests that were put into the prayer box and planning church events. Soon after, I was asked to join the Women's ministry board and facilitate one of the small groups at church. I felt like God was calling me to go out and encourage others, so in addition to small group, I would host get-togethers at my place for single women like me. I would share from the Word and we would share our struggles, triumphs and hard questions in a safe space. There were other single moms at church and we would often hang out and host sleepovers for our daughters at each other's homes.

Kiera was involved in Youth Ministry and sang her little sassy heart out in the children's choir. One morning, I woke up and she was in the living room watching a Mickey Mouse cartoon. She was about seven or eight at the time. In the cartoon, there was a sunrise scene which is the part where I walked in. As the sun rose on the television screen, Kiera, whose back was toward me, raised her arms and said "Hallelujah to the Holy Spirit" as if she too had discovered that she could find evidence of God's spirit and beauty in everything around her. I remember being so grateful, so overwhelmed by God's great grace and love for us.

In other areas of life, work was going great. I was working for a nonprofit, just like I'd always wanted, and to top it off, I had already received a promotion. While grad school was challenging, I absolutely loved learning and applying my course studies at work. I was also getting my finances together, which was a huge deal and something that I had often brought before God in prayer. Years of using my store credit cards irresponsibly so that I could engage in retail therapy had left my credit ailing. Now that I had been stable for a few years and splitting living expenses with Selina, I had created a budget that included giving, paying back debt and saving. Month by month, those balances were diminishing and I was able to pay for school out of pocket, pay off my car note and afford fun outings like trips to American Girl Place with Kiera. I also still shopped, but with cash and at a budgeted amount. I was and still am so good at stretching a budget with sales and discounts. I didn't pay full price for anything, but I was spiffy nonetheless!

> *I was like a tree that had been pruned and was now thriving and growing as I was planted firmly in the Lord. Did I get lonely? Oh, for sure!*

Not being vain, just stating that I was thriving in so many areas. It's okay to look and feel cute, ladies!

In 2006, our church choir began an annual summer trip to Spain where we would sing all over the northeast area of the country, spreading the Gospel. So, Kiera and I would have our spring break Florida vacation, and I would be able to travel for a couple of weeks during the summer to experience all of the beauty and history that Spain had to offer, all while sharing God's love. I am not sure what else I could have asked for in life at this point. I even had a good handle on my singleness because I had so many single friends and we all supported one another. Between 2005 and 2008, I was in a sweet spot of continued restoration and strengthening. Life was not perfect—as it never is—and neither was I, and I never will be, but there was a sweetness in abiding in God during that season. It was like Psalm 1:

> Blessed is the one
> who does not walk in step with the wicked
> or stand in the way that sinners take
> or sit in the company of mockers,
> but whose delight is in the law of the Lord,
> and who meditates on his law day and night.
> That person is like a tree planted by streams of water,
> which yields its fruit in season
> and whose leaf does not wither—
> whatever they do prospers. (Psalm 1:1–3 NIV)

I was like a tree that had been pruned and was now thriving and growing as I was planted firmly in the Lord. Did I get lonely? Oh, for sure! Did I ever meet men I would have liked to date? You'd better believe it! However, in my quiet time, God impressed something on me that I continually held on to. I wrote it down, held on to it in my heart, and used it as the standard for every counterfeit and distraction that would most certainly come my way.

First, it was that I needed to stop dating completely.

Secondly, the man He had for me would without a doubt be a man of God.

Thirdly, I would not need to pursue him. I would be pursued.

Lastly, there would not be any confusion about it.

After obtaining my Master's degree in 2007, I changed jobs once again and began working as a Senior Director in an arts organization in Harlem. Selina had moved out, and now it was just Kiera and me. I was financially in a place to comfortably support us both (thank God for rent control!) and life was all about Kiera, work, church, and friends. In 2008, I had changed positions again and was now working at a healthcare nonprofit that was closer to home. Two years of utter singleness is doable. Three is like getting a badge of honor, but after that, I started to be concerned. Kiera was getting older and had begun middle school. I was now thirty-one years old. The thirties are when many of us women suddenly start hearing clocks ominously ticking in the background of our daily lives. The novelty of the single life begins to wear thin. There were a couple of times in the past years when men were interested in me but nothing much resulted at all, mostly due to my non-interest, or the guidelines God had given me were not met. I had emerged unscathed, thankfully, because I had guarded my heart. But now my heart was longing to be opened and shared.

It was in 2008 that the weddings started. It was bound to happen. The first, and one of the most impacting, was when Josette got married on a sunny and clear day in June. Josette had waited longer than I had for this, and I was so happy for her. This wedding excitement was not just about celebrating with one of my very best friends, but it was an answer to a prayer that we, the Holy Home-girls, had been bringing before God for so long. I remember Wendy and I helped her to get ready that morning. Wendy did her hair and makeup. She glowed with utter exuberance. We prayed and rejoiced so much that day. I was the maid of honor and Wendy the matron of honor. I remember how much we danced and celebrated at that reception. However, after the wedding celebration was over, and the dress was hung up in my closet, the reality that my best friend was now married set in and I mourned a bit. I used to think nothing of calling Josette at any hour to vent or pray, and now I had to be cognizant and respectful that she was now a newlywed who needed time to adjust to her marriage and her new best friend.

Then there was Kiera's godmother Dana, who was a good friend since high school. Dana was such a doting godmother, starting with babysitting little baby Kiera in her dorm room when we were undergrads and I had to work. She worked for Disney for much of her career and there wasn't a year that she did not have a beautiful Disney princess costume for Kiera for her birthday, which also happens to be October 31st. Dana has always been an immense blessing to me, and Kiera and loves her with every fiber of her being. We had seen each other through some awful cringe-worthy relationships, but around the time that Greg and I dated a few years earlier, she met the man of her dreams, a man whom she had known since birth, go figure. There wasn't anything not to love about Anthony, a devoted and loving fiancé then, and an even more awesome husband and father today. None of us could have dreamed of anyone better for Dana. Kiera and I attended the wedding, which was beautiful, of course. I was asked to read 1 Corinthians 13 in the ceremony. I did so and read those words with all the passion and honor I could muster.

That same summer, my sorority sister Imelba, whom I pledged with and had been friends with since high school, also got married in a beautiful ceremony in Long Island. I got to hang out with my sorority sisters and had an amazing time celebrating her love. I think it was that fall when another one of my sorority sisters got married, this time at a modern New York City venue.

Also, in 2008, my younger brother—only by 18 months, but still younger—announced that he had proposed to his girlfriend, Jennifer. I was over-the-moon happy for him because Jenn was such a genuinely sweet ball of beautiful sunshine and she had taken my moody, goth style hermit brother and brought the very best out of him. Jenn has been a blessing to our family. Kiera, my younger sister and I were all in the wedding party, and I nearly fainted when I saw my brother dancing freely and with reckless abandon at his wedding. I don't think I had seen my brother dance since he tried his hand, unsuccessfully, at breakdancing back in 1985. He was one happy man!

On the night of Jenn's bachelorette party, she handed out

buttons to each of her bridesmaids. They had funny and sassy phrases like Diva, Wild one and such. She handed me my button and it said, "Always A Bridesmaid". Because I knew Jenn, I knew she would never intend me any offense, so I laughed it off. By this time, I had been in a couple of weddings and I could totally see how the shoe—or in this case, the button, fit. I laughed outwardly, but a narrative of doubt and discouragement sprung in my mind and began to take root. Was this what it was going to be like for me? Standing by as, two by two, those around me stepped into the phase of life I had been patiently waiting for?

On and on they went. Wedding after wedding, dress after dress. Even Selina—who passed notes to me during history in high school, which I still have—married her sweetheart, Shawn. I was just about the last single person left, and even those who were also single were at least in a relationship or dating. Now, can we be real about the struggle during seasons like this? Because I have spoken to other single women and I know that it's not easy, I want you to know this place of struggle is real. Don't beat yourself up over the myriad of thoughts that go through your mind. I was genuinely happy for my friends, I was. I was a darn good bridesmaid; I served my precious friends, planned showers and did hair and makeup. I was asked to pray at rehearsal dinners and at

> *God blessing others should be encouraging to us, not threatening. Testimonies should motivate us and fill us with hope, rather than deflate us.*

bridal showers. I infiltrated heaven with genuine prayers for love and blessings beyond measure. I also made sure that my friends got every cent worth spent on my plate by partying hard at those receptions—especially when that salsa and merengue came on!

Here is the other part of the narrative that is just as real but not as pretty. At the same time that I rejoiced with my friends, I also ached for myself. Why did it seem like everyone else was obtaining their heart's desire while I stood on the sidelines and cheered them on? I was so open about being in a place of waiting on God, and yet here I was being passed over again and again. I had surrendered everything, maintained obedience and purity, and yet it seemed like everyone else was enjoying their heart's desire except for me. Now let me say, this sort of thinking is so natural, but if unchecked, it can be dangerous. We can think that we are somehow owed blessings because of our behavior. But the fact is, even on my best day, I am still a sinner and I am woefully imperfect. I cannot allow myself to be in a position to think that my acts somehow mandate that God should do what I want Him to do. Our relationship with God should not be transactional. We do good, we get blessed. That type of thinking is treading on thin ice for sure. If we allow that mindset into our lives then as soon as we tire of waiting, or heaven forbid receive a "no" from God, we walk away from Him and into old behaviors.

A dangerous mindset I found myself struggling with during this season was the scarcity mindset. This is when we become discouraged every time someone else gets blessed because we think that somehow it means there is less blessing left over for us. A friend gets a good man, there are less around for me. Another gets a dream job, so that must mean that I will not. God blessing others should be encouraging to us, not threatening. Testimonies should motivate us and fill us with hope, rather than deflate us. What is for you is for you, and someone else getting what is for them in no way diminishes that truth. A scarcity mindset can lead to covetousness--fixating on what someone else has. When we do that, we miss all that we do have and, worse than that, we shrink God's power and creativity in our lives down to the size of our limited understanding. Do we think that God is not large enough to have plenty for all of His children? Is He not the Creator of the entire universe? Does He not know us all intimately down to the hairs on our head? Does he not have plans and purpose for us?

God's timing in our lives may not look like others timing. Our journeys will seldom mirror anyone else's journey but one thing I know is that God is creative. Just take a look at nature and how every flower is beautiful, but not the same as the next. They are different, but in no way is one less beautiful than the other. He is not a God of lack, He promised abundant life. But we have to let go of our own narrow notions of what abundant life is, and we most certainly need not measure our abundant life against someone else's.

I know that we don't want to have these thoughts. I never woke up one day and thought I would love to start comparing my life to that of others, and be stuck in sadness and gloom. But I also know that we are human beings, and these types of thoughts will rear their ugly heads. When they do, it is our responsibility is to cast them down and continue to speak God's truth right over them. There is no shame when these thoughts stop by, but it is so very dangerous to allow them to stay. We must be diligent to acknowledge bitter, jealous, self-defeating, comparison thoughts and aggressively cast them down. Moreover, we must actively pursue a change in our hearts—desiring to have a heart that's not fearful but one that trusts that God has amazing plans for us. After all, the Word says to guard our hearts above all else, for everything we do flows from it (Proverbs 4:23 NIV). So, how do we guard our hearts? By being in the Word, memorizing and meditating on scriptures that resonate with us, and prioritizing our relationship with God.

I was sad sometimes during this season of weddings. But the more I drew near to God, the less sad I was and the more hopeful I became. I strove to stay present in all moments from dress fittings to celebrations, so that I could share in the joy and excitement of the season instead of drifting away mentally and forecasting doom and gloom for myself. Realize that we do have a choice in how we allow circumstances to affect us. We need not succumb to bitterness, fear or disappointment. We can decide to take hold of joy and inexplicable peace, which Jesus told us that He gives (John 14:27).

Now, for those who need this message in a more direct manner, Girl, be happy for people! Especially your friends and loved ones! Be cognizant of how being sulky and withdrawn can be such a damper for what is one of the most important events in someone else's life. It is downright selfish to bring that into someone else's life-changing event. You wouldn't want someone doing it to you, would you? Sit at that single's table at the reception and smile. Refrain from critical comments. Get your Cha-Cha slide on! Be a light for all that you come into contact with, and have fun! Also, please try not to tackle or otherwise physically harm anyone if you are the type to go for the bouquet. Keep it classy!

There was a woman on my staff at work who I am still good friends with and absolutely adore to this day. Her name is Polina and she is such a presence. Tall and beautiful with an enchanting Russian accent. Polina has a way of disarming people and getting into personal conversations with even the most guarded of individuals. She just asked a lot of questions—very direct questions—and for some reason, I always felt obliged to answer. Early on in our time working together, Polina, who herself was married and had a son, asked about my love life and why I was single. I wish I had a dollar for every time I was asked that question. It would have given my retirement fund a healthy boost for sure.

"I just feel like God wants me to wait on what He has for me," I'd say matter-of-factly.

Polina, in her practical and well-meaning way, would encourage me to help God along by getting out there and dating. I'd respond with a "Thanks, but I am okay, I'm waiting on what God has for me." Then I'd promptly change the subject. As much as I wanted to communicate an answer that made total sense to people, nothing about faith makes sense. I knew that what I was choosing sounded bonkers to people, especially in the age of dating apps and speed dating events. There was no good human reason for me to not at least be dating. There was no cultural or societal standard that would prohibit me from getting out there and checking out my prospects, especially since I had a lot to offer.

Apparently, my singleness was very concerning because some months later, Polina told me that she had been talking on the phone to her mom, who was back in Uzbekistan, and told her about me and how much she loved working with me. When her mom ascertained that I was single despite all the wonderful qualities that Polina apparently saw in me and listed for her, her mother was at once alarmed and asked why I was not married. Polina of course reported this back to me in the hopes that wisdom from her mother would sway me. It did not, although I was so deeply

> *I believe that the enemy uses seemingly innocuous situations to quietly lure us away and have us stray from the right track, especially the closer we get to our breakthrough or blessing.*

honored and moved that Polina and her mom were so concerned for me and wanted good things for me.

A couple of friends took it further and just went ahead a few times and set me up to have coffee with Christian men who they knew and thought would be good options for me. I politely agreed, albeit a bit begrudgingly. If we compared them to the list I had, they would have ticked all of the boxes. Loved God, check. Pursuing me, check. No confusion—well, not on their end at least. However, these couple of coffee meet-ups did nothing for me. These were attractive, kind, established men who loved God and were genuinely into me. I wasn't into them though, which was slightly disappointing but not at all tragic.

One thing I did not want to do was to force myself into a relationship just because it seemed to make sense. That's hard when there isn't a glaring and dangerous reason not to keep going. But just because something isn't glaring and dangerous does not mean that it's a green light to go ahead. Some things are just not beneficial for us. Moreover, I believe that the enemy uses seemingly innocuous situations to quietly lure us away and have us stray from the right track, especially the closer we get to our breakthrough or blessing. An opportunity or person seems harmless; it looks a lot like the promise that God has given us. The counterfeit looks so real that we begin to convince ourselves we can work around the other parts that don't quite line up with the promise. Just because a man was a single, responsible, God-loving adult, and I was also a single, responsible God-loving adult, did not mean we would have made a good union. I don't know about you, but if I am going to wait on what God has for me and suffer through seasons of discomfort and loneliness, then I want the best that I can get out of it, not some 'almost good enough'. The God we serve is not a God of 'almost good enough'. He is a God of *It is good* (Genesis 1:31). He knows and can deliver what is BEST for us, not just 'pretty good'. God is not a God of mediocrity, so don't settle when waiting on what He has for you. Wait on the very best.

One of my friends from church, Charity, who was a few years younger than I was and an aspiring Broadway star (she has an amazing Broadway career now), began living with Kiera and me. The term 'starving artist' is REAL, and I was so happy for the opportunity to be a blessing to someone. I was also excited to have another grown up in the house to talk to. Kiera loved and admired Charity so much. For her, having someone in their early twenties around was so much cooler than a mom teetering on thirty. There was just ministry and girl power all over my home. I would encourage Charity, pray with her through her life challenges and choices and she would do the same for me. God sent me companionship during a time when loneliness really could have taken a dark hold on me. I could choose to be grateful or wallow in what I felt I lacked. I chose to enjoy girl time to the fullest!

I felt like the many Bible verses that talk about being tested and refined by fire were resonating with me. It was not a pleasant process. The more I stayed in that fire and let God do His work in me, the more the years of lies, shame, loneliness and putting my hope in people and not God were being drained from me...much like the impurities that are drained from gold in the hottest of fires. I shared this with Charity, including how—although it was often difficult—I knew in my spirit I would come out as pure gold just like the Bible said. No matter what I saw, what I felt or what people with all of their good intentions spoke over me with their limited vantage points, I would come out on the other side of this season gleaming. Whether or not I would have a ring gleaming on my finger or not wasn't the point. I would be gleaming with being secure in God's love, abundance and purpose. This was just pure faith talk, no tangible evidence at all, just a security in my spirit that I would be more than okay. Our conversations over delicious cups of coffee and prayers in agreement were like a balm to my soul. Charity gave me a card for one of my birthdays and in it, she addressed me as "Pazit", the Hebrew word for gold. She was believing with me.

FOOD *for* THOUGHT

"Finally, brothers and sisters, whatever is true, whatever is noble, whatever is right, whatever is pure, whatever is lovely, whatever is admirable—if anything is excellent or praiseworthy—think about such things. Whatever you have learned or received or heard from me, or seen in me—put it into practice. And the God of peace will be with you." (Philippians 4:8–9 NIV)

- Are there any areas in your life where you feel that God has overlooked you? How does that make you feel? Be brutally honest with yourself and write it down. Instead of dwelling on what you think is missing in your life, focus on what you do have. Write down what you can be grateful for here.

- Is there something that God is calling you to do that is so counterculture that it looks foolish? How can you be strengthened to stay the course?

PART THREE

True Love

CHAPTER *Eight*

A NEW SEASON

ven as it seemed that my love life was at a perpetual stand-
still, God had a way of keeping things exciting for me. One
thing that my life was not throughout any of these years was
stagnant. In 2009, I received a call from Pastor Bobby. He wanted
to meet with me to talk about something huge. A small group of
us met at City Diner on 92nd street and Broadway, not far from our
church. He shared that he had been called to start a new church and
wanted to extend the invitation for me to be one of the founding
congregants. This was huge indeed.

I would leave the church that had become a second home to
me. The place where I had experienced exponential growth in my
relationship with God and the place where I was now serving God
and encouraging others in their own relationships. This was the only
church Kiera had ever known. This was also the church where I had
lived through a pretty significant heartbreak and come out on the
other side, changed for the better. I was forever changed because I
walked into that church and practically ran up the altar many years
before. It was also no question to me that Pastor Bobby had been
used in such a mighty way in my life and was an integral part of my

growth during those years. He had encouraged me, instructed me in the Word, shown by example what it meant to live a life that sought after and honored God, and he had also brought me into the fold of a community that I never thought I was worthy of.

This would be a significant transition for Kiera and me. Would I possibly be leaving friends to go on this new venture? Yes. Would it feel different to worship elsewhere, especially since there was not even a building? Sure. Would this be a fresh start, perhaps the fresh start I needed to move into the next season that God had for me? Oh yes!

In April, 2009, New Light Baptist Church of Greater New York City had its first service in a living room. There were about twenty of us. The location and number of those gathered did not matter one bit though; we knew the church was not merely a breathtaking edifice. The stained-glass windows of the church do not go out and share the good news. Ornate pulpits only provide a physical platform, but the Word has to come forth from a follower of God. So, there we were, ready for what God would have us do. Who knew what God would have in store for me?

We rented out a school auditorium for our Sunday services, and our first official service was that Easter Sunday. I had invited friends and colleagues who did not have church homes, and family members too. What was even better was that my close friends were also part of the new church. I still have pictures from that day posing, cheerfully with Josette and Wendy, my tried and true Holy Homegirls. I have another of me holding Wendy's newest baby in one arm and a former coworker's baby in the other. My mom and dad had joined as well. Some of the young women I mentored also had come over. The crisp and sunny early spring weather was like a reflection of the jubilation that my heart felt on this day. It truly felt like a new season was beginning on all fronts.

Someone else had stopped by our service to check things out. Can you guess who? I am so very proud to report to you that although Greg came by and we greeted one another—that was it for me! No longing, no sadness, no bitterness, no bathroom floors! I greeted him and kept it moving. I gave thanks for all that God had put into my hands instead of lamenting that which had been allowed to slip away. I was not the same woman I was six years before. I had confidence in who I was in God. I knew beyond a shadow of a doubt that I was God's precious daughter and He had good plans in store for me. I could not hold people in prison for rejecting me. I could actually be grateful that their rejection catapulted me into the greatest and purest acceptance I have ever known. Their rejection flung me into the arms of my loving Father.

> *I had confidence in who I was in God. I knew beyond a shadow of a doubt that I was God's precious daughter and He had good plans in store for me. I could not hold people in prison for rejecting me.*

That evening, Kiera and I left on our annual Florida vacation. We stayed once more with my sorority sister and her daughter. God extended even more grace upon me so that now, this sorority sister

whom I had been visiting for years, was now also in her own beautiful relationship with God. We talked about the goodness of God over
delicious cups of coffee and lifted each other up in prayer, asking
God to cover and protect our girls and to keep us in His will. It
was an amazingly sweet time. Probably the only similarity between
returning home from my vacation back in 2004 and now was that I
had an awesome tan. What was different was that this time, I came
back without any misplaced confidence about who would be fulfilling my hopes and dreams. I was a blank slate, rested and ready to
take on whatever God had in store, knowing that He is completely
trustworthy and faithful.

When I returned from vacation, we began rehearsals for our
upcoming trip to Spain that summer. I was excited to return to
Spain for the fourth time. I was looking forward to singing in open
town squares and old theaters, to the beauty of the architecture,
rich history, small town festivals that were like something out of a
movie, our wonderful friends in Spain, and most of all, quiet devotions at a quiet table on a cobblestone street enjoying delicious
Spanish coffee! Oh, the coffee! I often wish I could be transported
back to those moments of Jesus and coffee under the Spanish sun.
While our friends in Spain considered it such a blessing for us travel
to their county to share the Gospel, we were so immensely blessed
by the experience as well.

At the end of one of our rehearsals, Pastor Bobby began to
introduce those who would be coming along on our Spain trip to
support the choir. I turned around for a quick look and saw Greg

standing there. I wasn't sure what to think. I guess he was coming over to the new church as well. I quickly turned back around and made conversation with the person next to me. The day we traveled to Spain was a long one. We had a layover in Paris. I found some delicious French coffee at the airport and enjoyed traveling with Charity, Josette and other good friends. Greg and I hardly said anything past hello to one another, and I wondered if he was leery of me. I mean, in the past I had been quite short and sometimes rude to him in an effort to protect myself. I wasn't in that bitter space anymore, but I also was not trying to make myself vulnerable. I wanted to guard my heart above all else.

In Spain, there was a lot of walking to and from venues as well as long rides into various small towns and cities. Besides singing, there was a lot of time to be social and take in the sights and culture of whatever city we were in. We would split into smaller groups of close friends. Charity and I enjoyed so much coffee and gelato. It was sublime. We strolled past shops and I remember seeing a bridal shop called Pronovias with beautiful gowns in the window.

"When I get married, I am getting my dress from this store," I announced to Charity. I didn't mind that there was no wedding in sight. I could dream and let it be just that—a beautiful dream that I was trusting God to do as He pleased with.

Greg and I had many good friends in common like Beatrice and others. So, it was perfectly natural that as the days went on, casual conversation sprung up and the cold uneasiness of years of not having interacted quickly melted away to reveal two people who still enjoyed being around each other. We visited old Castilla's (castles) and Greg would begin to quote lines from the Lord of the Rings. We caught up on how we had been doing and where we were professionally. One evening, we were the only two people interested in watching Clash of the Titans in the hotel courtyard. Who doesn't love old 80's sci-fi? I guess that would be most of our friends. With all the expectations of a relationship stripped away, we just enjoyed hanging out.

One evening, we were in the hotel lobby talking about what God had done in our lives over the past years. There is something about late night conversation that diminishes our defenses. Perhaps it's because we are tired. Perhaps we felt more hidden and protected in dimmed lighting. In any case, we talked for a few hours in that lobby until it was just us and the front desk staff who were left. A quiet pause emerged as it seemed we had nothing left to say. As I began to realize how late it was and started to get up to go to my room, he began to talk. He told me he deeply respected and cared for me and that he always had. He admitted that things could have gone better with how we ended things and he apologized for ever hurting me. I also apologized for acting bitterly toward him. Then I went to my room, grabbed Charity, who was my roommate at the hotel, and cried happy tears with her.

> *Forgiveness does not require that those who offend us ever make amends. Forgiveness is something that we decide to embrace even in the midst of offense.*

Until that moment on the trip, Greg and I had pretty much not acknowledged that we ever even knew each other before. We hung out with our friends and shopped in the local shops and ate at the local cafes and took in the amazing Spanish sunshine and laughed—a lot. But we could have been two people who had just met. There was no depth. We just glazed over the past like it never happened and I honestly was happy to do so. I didn't want to dredge up anything uncomfortable or have drama during one of my favorite times and in one of my favorite places of all time. I just wanted to move forward. But part of moving forward healthily was making peace with the past.

Forgiveness does not require that those who offend us ever make amends. Forgiveness is something that we decide to embrace even in the midst of offense. Even if the other person has no intention whatsoever of apologizing or admitting wrongdoing, we forgive because it's part of our own healing and freedom. I love a saying from one of my favorite preachers that says, "Unforgiveness is like drinking poison and expecting the other person to die." Forgiveness is just as much for us as it is for those who have hurt us. I had forgiven Greg years prior to that moment in a dimly lit and quiet hotel lobby in Spain. Perhaps that moment was not just about forgiveness, perhaps it was also about taking responsibility. It's so easy to think that everything is all good and at peace so there is no need to be real about the past. When we are covered by grace and forgiven so freely by God, it's easy to just keep going without parking at the uncomfortable place of acknowledgment and repentance. But unless we do acknowledge our behavior and commit to doing better next time, we may find ourselves right back at God's feet with the same issues. It was a big step for Greg, I think, to bring up and apologize for the past. It was freeing for me to take responsibility for my less than gracious countenance. I think we had both already forgiven but there was healing in taking responsibility for our actions. It cleared the air for us to maybe truly move forward as friends.

We faced the rest of the trip on a truly new note. Of course, there were those few people who made comments and sly jokes about Greg and I having such a great rapport during the trip. One evening, a group of us planned to go out to dinner. We had come from spending the afternoon at a local pool, and planned to meet up after getting refreshed. I wore a simple black cotton maxi dress and flat sandals. Simple but chic. When we met in the hotel lobby, Greg had changed into a cream-colored linen top and beige slacks. Everyone else was wearing jeans or shorts with casual tops. Needless to say, this garnered smarty pants comments about us having planned this and going on a date, which we both vehemently denied. There was no need to make this all something that it wasn't. It's quite funny how adults can so quickly begin acting like middle-school kids! It didn't bother me though. I was just grateful to have turned a corner and to have met the Greg that God had developed over the years. Same funny and intelligent person, but a new creature in Christ at the same time. Bitterness and unforgiveness would have had me miss out on that.

FOOD *for* THOUGHT

"Get rid of all bitterness, rage and anger, brawling and slander, along with every form of malice. Be kind and compassionate to one another, forgiving each other, just as in Christ God forgave you." (Ephesians 4:31–32 NIV)

- Is there unforgiveness in your heart toward someone?
- Do you need to accept responsibility and make amends with someone? Don't delay in either of these areas.

CHAPTER *Nine*

VIVA ESPAÑA

I was back in New York and enjoying the rest of the summer, my favorite season. One Saturday, Kiera and I were at the beach. She was eleven and we were lying on the blanket, chatting between long pauses of napping and daydreaming. Kiera would often ask for a sibling and I would tell her that it would only happen if God brought me a husband. No husband, no sibling. On this day, as we lay in the middle of Orchard Beach in the Bronx, with the mixed sounds of salsa, hip-hop and R&B wafting about us, she shared that she wanted a dad. This was hard since I wanted to give Kiera all that she needed and most of what she wanted if it was within reason. Why shouldn't a young girl want a dad of her own? Kiera had been very blessed to have so many male figures who had stepped in to help me raise her, like my dad, brother and even Pastor Bobby. They had provided love, protection, and even some spoiling. I knew though, that it was not the same as having your own dad, and I knew that there was really nothing that I could, or rather, should do about it. I felt a tinge of failure creeping in and redirected her to the same place where I would often have to redirect myself.

"You have to ask God about that," I said.

Long pause.

"You know who I wouldn't mind having for a dad, if you were to marry someone?"

"Who?" I asked, a little afraid of what the answer could be. It could be anyone from a rapper to one of her teachers.

"Greg. He's always been so nice to me." Good grief, could no one leave well enough alone? Even my own child?

"Yeah, you have to talk to God about that," I responded again, certain that only God would be able to maneuver such an outcome.

I was called to another meeting with Pastor Bobby. He told me that he wanted me to be ordained as a minister in the church and also lead the Women's ministry. You do realize who he was talking to, right? You did read the book all the way through up until now and realize that this was nothing I ever could have imagined, right? If I were to go back in time pretty much to any time prior to this day, and tell myself that I would be ministering to women as an ordained minister, I would have laughed heartily and indignantly. In that moment when Pastor Bobby told me though, it felt right to me. Not because I wanted to be a minister because I was not even sure what that meant. Not because I thought I was qualified, because it is so obvious that I was not. I had already been ministering to women for years, both in and out of church. God allowed this to come naturally to me. I was having small groups with women from my church, facilitating lunchtime Bible studies with the young women on my staff at work and regularly providing counsel and encouragement to women in my friends and family. Not for titles, not for reward, not for anything except desperately wanting other women to know that sweet love and freedom that I had found in Him. I never forced my faith on anyone, it was just God moving and using me as He pleased. It's what I truly and deeply love to do. Win, win.

There was a cohort of us who had been chosen for servant leadership roles in the church. Some would be pastors, others ministers, and also deacons. We would meet for class every week and have to complete assignments and go through a vetting process down in Virginia Beach at Pastor Bobby's father's church, which was our oversight church. If nothing else, becoming ordained and wearing a collar would certainly heighten suspicions for many who had thought over the years that I was becoming some kind of nun!

As is turned out, both Josette and Wendy were also being ordained, and so was my pal Greg. Let's pause here for a minute because I do not want to gloss over this move of God. Sister, I promise you that never in a million years did I think that the guy that I was dating would get saved, start serving God, and that he and I would both be getting ordained and be friends seven years down the line. It

> *Never stop being in awe of what God has done. My sister, no matter how seemingly big or small the move, God is working in your life.*

sounds way too farfetched, and frankly doesn't sound like the kind of dream I'd even want to be having. None of this was my hope or dream when I surrendered to God. Greg, a pastor? Me, a minister? Holy Homegirls, ordained too? Well, that part I could have seen coming. But certainly not me and not Greg. I never want to lose the wonder of what God has done in my life. I never want to take for granted any of the flat-out miracles that God has performed.

When I stop being amazed at how God took me in as His own and changed me; when I stop being amazed at His love, how He draws me close, how He orchestrates my life—a life I never could have designed on my own—when my awe for God loses its luster or worse, when I forget how far God has brought me, and when I start taking credit for what He has done, then I am treading on dangerous soil. Never stop being in awe of what God has done. My sister, no matter how seemingly big or small the move, God is working in your life. It's easy to take on a "What have you done for me lately?" attitude with God. It's easy to behave as if He owes us something—that He has to keep proving His power and love for us. He does not. Yet, in all of his grace and mercy for us, He still does have plans. But those plans are kept on a need-to-know basis. I certainly did not need to know that God had this planned all along. I likely would have run away - or worse, tried to execute God's plan in my own power.

Greg would also be leading the Men's ministry. Having had many conversations with him at our new church about God, the Word and hearing his insights and heart for God during our Wednesday night Bible studies, it was undeniable that he had developed a deeper love and commitment to serving God. None of us had seen this coming, but God saw this even as we were being knit together in our mother's wombs. Speaking of mothers, can you imagine how my mother was during this season? Here was her child for whom she prayed fervently. How many times had she become discouraged by my behavior and poor choices? How many times must she have begun to lose heart because it took me SO LONG to surrender myself over to God? Yet, she kept praying, kept bringing me before the throne. I suppose not even she knew that God had this much in mind. More than we can ask or think for sure.

The next months were filled with planning women's events, studying, leadership meetings and continuing to get professionally and financially stable. Up to this point, I had been renting in the same building that my parents lived in and while it was beyond convenient and helpful to have moral support, free babysitting and home cooked dinners on those nights when I was so busy with school at my regular disposal, I began to feel like perhaps I needed to spread my wings soon. I started researching what it would take to buy a condo in the next couple of years and saved money more aggressively. I had been out of debt for some time and enjoyed being able to be generous and also meeting Kiera's and my own needs with plenty of shoe shopping—I mean, little treats here and there.

A new rhythm had set in where a big group of us would go out to eat after service on Sundays. I didn't have a car at the time and Greg would often offer to give me and Kiera a ride home since we were on the way downtown. While I was so pleased about the new-found friendship that we had, I also could not deny that this man was still as attractive as ever. Actually more...more attractive. I don't just mean broad shoulders and a gorgeous smile either. When this man spoke about God and broke down the Word, it was mesmerizing to me. Greg had always been so intelligent and eloquent, but adding the anointing of the Holy Spirit and an open and contagious love for God was just over the top. It was hard to keep my mind steady and not imagine that there could be more. However, I knew that going mentally down that road would not be helpful and could ruin all the progress being made.

I often think of trials as tests. The first couple of times, we may fail at handling what comes our way out of sheer ignorance or defiance. Then, there can be a reprieve from the situation where we are essentially taken to school. For me, it was the years of having distractions in the form of a man removed, focusing on my relationship with God and studying His Word. During those years, I devoured scripture, Bible studies, books and teachings and in theory, I began to know what was right. There is something though about amassing knowledge without practicing what you have learned. It can puff us up and make us think that we are somehow beyond making the same mistakes again. We examine our former missteps and agree wholeheartedly about the places where we could have done better. We even imagine going back and handling it differently. We have gone so long without even being in that situation, however, that we don't remember how hard it actually is to be in it and make wise decisions. However, if we have been studying diligently, if we have been continually in God's presence and if we are on alert and sober-minded, knowing that we have an enemy that is looking to trip us up, then we have a fighting chance when that test comes back around. Because it will.

So, this was my test. Becoming friends—true friends—with the person whom I could not even be around at one point. It would have been easier if he had halitosis or otherwise repelled me but, as I've said, it was quite the opposite. We were now becoming co-laborers for God's Kingdom, so it wasn't like I could get out of being around him. No, there was no avoidance tactic to be employed here. God wanted me to face this head-on and reflect back to Him, through my thoughts and actions, what He had been pouring into me. He wanted me to face a new and improved version of what had tripped me up before and choose Him this time around. Not only did this feel like I test but it seemed like somehow I ended up in the AP version! I truly did not want to go back to the places I had been delivered from, but wanting something and acting like you want it are two different things. I knew that being passive and just wanting to make better decisions would not keep me grounded in God. I would have to make the choice to honor God, one at a time, repeatedly.

Later that fall, almost our entire congregation traveled down to Virginia Beach for the weekend of our ordination. Besides church members, family and friends of those being ordained also made the trip to witness and celebrate what God was doing. There is always such a fun element to traveling to Virginia Beach. Well, not so much the ride on a charter bus, because I notoriously get motion sickness. However, once off the road, it was like arriving at our second home. The church in Virginia Beach always shows us the epitome of southern hospitality. We, being New Yorkers, delight ourselves in having a Waffle House walking distance to the church and hotel where we stay. Also, no trip is ever complete without taking up the entire back row of tables at the local Golden Corral and stuffing ourselves.

I had traveled down to VA Beach many times before with the Ensemble and also for Pastor Bobby's ordination. This time was totally different. I would be set apart as a servant not only of God, but His people. I didn't take this lightly and still do not. I was well aware that I was not taking on this new role to have a title and wear a specific outfit, or to be served by people. I would be submitting myself and making myself available to serve others.

More specifically, I was tasked with the care and discipleship of God's precious daughters. I did not know why God had chosen this for me. I know I was not qualified. I had a past. I was a single mom. I wasn't some learned Bible scholar. I was so flawed, and still am. Anyone looking at me would dismiss me and have good reason to do so. In spite of all the reasons that no one would choose me, God did. That's His pleasure. 1 Corinthians 1:27 says that God uses the foolish things of the world to shame the wise. I love the Message translation which says:

> *He will use vessels that look so woefully unlikely, so wrong for the job, without pedigree or anything to boast about, so that people will know, beyond a shadow of a doubt, that it could be no one but God who called and equipped them.*

Take a good look, friends, at who you were when you got

called into this life. I don't see many of "the brightest and the best" among you, not many influential, not many from high-society families. Isn't it obvious that God deliberately chose men and women that the culture overlooks and exploits and abuses, chose these "nobodies" to expose the hollow pretensions of the "somebodies"? That makes it quite clear that none of you can get by with blowing your own horn before God. Everything that we have—right thinking and right living, a clean slate and a fresh start—comes from God by way of Jesus Christ. That's why we have the saying, "If you're going to blow a horn, blow a trumpet for God." (1 Corinthians 1:27–31 MSG)

I take such comfort in the fact that I am the foolish thing, and there is no reason to hide it. I am so imperfect, and God choosing to use me has less to do with my capabilities and qualifications, and more to do with the fact that He just wants to get the glory. He will use vessels that look so woefully unlikely, so wrong for the job, without pedigree or anything to boast about, so that people will know, beyond a shadow of a doubt, that it could be no one but God who called and equipped them.

If you have ever counted yourself out of a move of God in your life; if you have ever not even tried, or you have been hiding and trying to evade what God wants to do through you because of the shame of your past, or because you are a woman, or because you just don't feel like you measure up, or because you have been drinking from the poisonous fountain of comparison, then it is my sincere prayer that you read my story and understand that God is so much bigger—His plans so much more mind blowing and irrational than what you feel or what you tell yourself. Trust God! Trust that He may be bringing you to new and scary places, but that He is with you. The more unlikely a candidate you are for the task ahead, the more glory He brings to Himself by placing you there and then doing a mighty work through you. What disciple could have possibly been worthy to travel with and learn from Jesus and carry on His legacy? They were a hot mess. And so am I. And so are you. Messy and called! Stay focused on God and keep it moving anyway. To Him be the glory!

There was a guest bishop who came to preach at our ordination. For those of you who are asking who or what is a bishop, well a bishop is like a more experienced, higher-up leader in some churches. But don't get stuck on titles, the good part comes next. His message was about the widow in 1 Kings 17, whom Elijah came upon as she was gathering sticks. There was a drought in the land, people were going hungry and the outlook seemed grim. Elijah, as instructed by the Lord, asked the widow to bring him some bread to eat, to which she informed him that all she had left in the world was a little bit of flour and oil that so that she and her son could have one final meal before they die. Yikes. If you read on in the story, you will see that the widow used that last little bit she had, the bit she just knew would be her last, to make bread for Elijah as well as for her and her son. What she thought was her last point, the beginning of her demise, ended up being the very place where she was able to witness God's power and authority. She was able to dip again and again into that container of flour, and where there should have been nothing left, God provided more. She was able to eat for days from provision that should have already expired. This is my paraphrase of the passage and certainly not a play-by-play synopsis of the bishop's sermon that day, but one phrase that I do remember clearly was when he told us not to be afraid to bake our cake. Even if it seemed we were at our last and there was nothing left on the horizon, God would honor that act of obedience.

There are times when I hear a message and file it away for another day. There are times when a message does not resonate with me at all, or when I admittedly think of someone else for whom the message would be perfect. There, in that service, surrounded by hundreds of other people, I knew that the word was for me. I felt like my dreams, my habits, my desires were the very last thing that I could hold on to. The outcome for me was death because the wages of sin is death. Perhaps not physical death but I believe my life, the way I was living prior to trusting God was leading me to the death of all of the promise that the little girl at Church camp had all those years before. When God pursued me, He asked me to give those things over to Him, to take my very last hopes and surrender them. Would there be more for me after giving everything away to God? My heart was so sure that God was telling me not to give up giving of myself, that I would not reach my end, but a new beginning in Him.

FOOD *for* THOUGHT

- What was the last thing God told you to do but you haven't done it? Be honest, what has stopped you?
- It's not too late to move forward, even if you feel fear. Trust that God will give you all that you need along the way, but you have to start moving. What is a first step you can take?

CHAPTER Ten

ARE YOU READY FOR THIS?

O ne of our church's mission commitments was to Haiti. There was a family in our church who had a house out there and wanted it to be used for ministry. We were scheduled to go to Haiti in late spring and were all astounded when, in January, 2010, a major earthquake devastated the country and killed hundreds of thousands of people. The house we were planning to transform into a clinic was reduced to rubble. After much prayer, we decided that we would still travel to Haiti early that May to help where we could and assess the damage to the home. I was so excited for another overseas missions' trip, this one so vastly different than my many trips to Spain.

About six of us traveled to Haiti, including all of our pastors. Haiti was everything that I thought it would be but more. There was a resilience I had never seen before in the people we met. In spite of how damaged and void of infrastructure the country was, I still saw so much beauty in both the land and people. Like so many places I had been, there was such a hospitality and kindness extended to us and it was so humbling. Where the grand house had once stood, small cabins were built to house us. On our first evening there, after dinner, we sat in the open air and sang and prayed. Greg shared a devotion and as he closed, nightfall closed around us, turning everything into a deep ebony and setting the stage for stars like I have never seen. There isn't much more humbling than sitting in the dark under the majesty of stars that God hung in the universe. I couldn't believe the experiences that God was allowing me to have. While I was heartbroken about the poverty and hurt all around me, I was also so grateful for an opportunity to join Him in whatever way He deemed on this trip.

I quickly took to one young woman named Chantal who worked in the house where we stayed. She had such a quiet and graceful way about her, and her boyfriend was a young man who also worked at the house. I'd spend time in the kitchen area just watching and listening to the women and marveling at their strength and contentment. I am an avid people watcher, so this was like bliss to me.

One afternoon after a busy morning, we had some downtime and were staying cool in one of the cabins. We were all chatting until one by one, the others flitted off and it was just Greg and me. We talked for hours. I wish I could remember what it was about, but little details emerge here and there. I remember him saying he really wasn't sure he would ever be with someone again or if he would find the person for him. I told him to stop speaking so negatively and making long-term decisions based on temporary feelings. God could do anything. The rest of the conversation was just that easy banter filled with humor and random things in common that we always shared. Greg was leaving the trip before the rest of us to attend a close friend's wedding over in the Dominican Republic. He'd be the best man. I could totally relate.

Before leaving Haiti, I found out that Chantal was engaged, and I was over the moon happy for her. Love in the midst of tragedy is a message, loud and clear, that we can still keep going in spite of circumstances that try to destroy us. Love, laughter and family would keep going.

We landed at Kennedy airport and I turned my phone on after five days of being disconnected. In buzzed the text messages.

My mom: "Let us know when you land."

Greg: "Let me know when you land."

O-kay...nothing strange there. Family and friends ensuring my safe return. I texted them both back that I had landed.

The next day, Greg texted me asking me to go out to Jamba Juice. He wanted to show me the pictures from the wedding he attended. That evening, I took the ride with him and we sat in his car while he went through the pictures one by one, giving me details on who was who, the room he stayed, the resort, and food. It sounded like a really great time. Then he dropped me off at home. We prayed and parted ways.

By this time, Greg and I were communicating pretty regularly and I kept casting down those pesky imaginations when they would creep up. But they would creep a little more than before. At that point I realized that I needed accountability partners in this with me. Although I knew to be still and wait on God, I also knew that I could use reinforcements bombarding heaven on my behalf. Our friendship was just that, a friendship, and I really enjoyed it. I enjoyed our conversations, praying together, and also having a male friend to talk to. But I also had feelings that were more, and I had to be honest about it and get prayer and counsel to make sure that I did not regress.

"Stay focused girl, you've come too far to slip up now," I would tell myself.

My community of accountability partners included the Holy Homegirls, of course, as well as Charity and one more mature woman whom I knew to be a prayer warrior. My prayer? God please keep me grounded, keep things clear, and guard my heart. One thing these women did not do was give me false hope or cosign any hint of foolishness on my part. Some days were a breeze and I would be fine. Other days I would have to confess thoughts that I entertained and just pray again to be grounded, clear-headed and to guard my heart.

On Mother's Day, my siblings, Kiera and I took my mom to a brunch. There were lots of other people from church there, as it was catered and hosted by Selina and her sister. A couple of tables over were Greg and his mom, who had come up to visit from Florida. I had met his mom briefly years ago at our other church and gotten to see her again at our ordination. Greg texted me about halfway through the brunch, asking what we would be doing next. I texted back that we didn't have any other plans, so he invited us to the movies with him and his mom. I didn't stop to examine how random this was, I just asked my mom if she'd like to go to the movies and she agreed. So, Greg, his mom, my mom, Kiera, and I all went to the movies to see the latest Iron Man movie. Our moms were very similar and hit it off immediately. I'm not sure either of them was into the movie—I felt they were trying hard not to look puzzled or confused. Puerto Rican mom poker face—a very hard skill to exhibit indeed.

This, of course, went straight to my prayer/accountability partners. I did not even want to try to make sense of why Greg would want to spend Mother's Day with us. I tried anyway. Maybe he saw me like a sister. That was it. Maybe we had grown so close that I was like his sister. One certainly does spend Mother's Day with their sisters. I had just been with my own sister earlier that day. Sister Lydia, that made sense.

Two people were not trying to hear this theory and were vocal about it. Polina and one of my prayer warriors. Polina, who made sure she stayed in the know about all things concerning me, playfully called Greg "Snow Pal",

If nothing else, I felt like I was being tested. Would I be able to trust God and be still with so much going on in and around me? Would I wait for how He said my blessing would come, or would I try and hurry him along and make a drastic mistake in the process?

because earlier that winter, she ascertained that he and I communicated all day via text on a snow day. From the outside eye looking in, she would be right in assuming that there was more to this. It looked like two people growing closer and closer to each other and spending increasingly more time together, texting and checking in with one another during lunch, on their way to their respective gym sessions after work, and a little more before dinner. It looked like something more. But I fought that with everything that I had. My prayer warrior was surprisingly blunter.

"Girl, just buy your dress," she would say, so matter-of-factly.

"Sigh, no, this is not that kind of thing. We are just really good friends and I need to accept that fully and not want anything more."

"Like I said, go buy your dress."

This really intensified when we returned from Haiti. Before, I was really at peace with the fact that we were friends, and that God would chill the every-now-and-then thoughts of more. Now, it was like suspicion was rising, and for good reason. Before, when we were friends, Greg seemed to shut me out of parts of his life and communicated with me less and less. Now, it was the opposite. In the midst of all this, I had to stay really focused. We were a few weeks away from our first women's retreat, and my plate was full.

A couple of weeks before Memorial Day, Greg asked me to start fasting and praying with him as he was going to be bringing the message on the Sunday before Memorial Day. As part of the fast, he also wanted to cut our evening phone calls so we could focus on prayer and Bible study. I was actually quite relieved at this suggestion because it would give me a chance to get my wits back about me. The past couple of weeks had been filled with daydreaming and speculation, but, thankfully, prayer and obedience as well. I think that's when obedience is at its most potent. If nothing else, I felt like

I was being tested. Would I be able to trust God and be still with so much going on in and around me? Would I wait for how He said my blessing would come, or would I try and hurry him along and make a drastic mistake in the process? Wait on the Lord; be strong and take heart, and wait on the Lord. Fasting and prayer were just what I needed.

That sermon that Greg preached that last Sunday in May was powerful and anointed. It was such a blessing, and I remember thinking how it seemed Greg was made for this. Many of us had made plans to go over to our friends' house, the Zlatkin's, after church for a barbeque. Jesse and Malika Zlatkin had become good friends of mine after our second trip to Spain, and Kiera loved hanging out with their kids. As we were walking out of church, Pastor Bobby stopped Greg and me. He wanted to have a meeting with us later that night to talk about some vision for the men's and women's ministry. He asked if we could meet at a local Starbucks at 9pm, and we agreed.

We also had one more stop to make at a cook-out that a couple from our church was having on the Upper West Side. We stopped by for a little while to fellowship, and as we left, they mentioned what good a couple Greg and I made.

"Oh no, we are not a couple at all, just friends," I said as soberly as I could. Greg remained silent. I nervously giggled as we got into the elevator.

"I'm so sorry about that. I don't know why they would think that," I said quickly for damage control. I was so enjoying our friendship and didn't want it tarnished because people made more of it than it was.

"It's cool, it's cool," he said nonchalantly.

"Okay, cool," I said as I exhaled in relief.

We hung out at the Zlatkins the rest of that afternoon, Greg mainly on the deck with the guys, Kiera off with the Zlatkin kids, and I in the kitchen chatting it up with my friends. As evening progressed, Greg gave me a nod through the screen door indicating that we should get a move on. I sat quietly in the car as we drove back to Manhattan. I had a really good day, from that morning's service to all of the fellowship. I was grateful that I felt at peace and level-headed. If there was never anything more between me and Greg, this was enough. We stopped by my mom's house to drop off Kiera for a couple of hours or so, while we met with Pastor Bobby.

The Starbucks wasn't too far on 87th and Lexington Avenue. Pastor Bobby was already inside waiting for us at a table. I sat down, took out my notebook and opened it, ready to glean from whatever he had to share. After Greg ordered our drinks, he went to the restroom. When he came back, he looked weird and flustered. Just as I was ready for Pastor to start speaking, Greg started.

"I just want you to know that you have been such an important part of my life. It was because of you that I started my relationship with God and for that I am forever grateful," he said to me.

"Thank you," I replied sincerely, again glad for how this had all shaped up.

Greg continued, "Over the years, God has had to do some work in each of us and we are not the same people we were before, but I am so grateful for that."

I nodded in agreement. This was cool, but I was wondering when Pastor would interrupt him so our meeting could begin. We were here on official business.

"Over these past months, I've been able to get to know you again as the woman you are now, and you have become a friend to me. You've become my best friend."

Ah, so this was what he was getting at! He was taking this opportunity, with Pastor Bobby as witness, to ensure that I knew we were friends and only friends. That comment earlier must have gotten to him. I had a feeling it would.

At this, I nodded more vehemently and looked at Pastor Bobby, who was just nodding as well. Just when I started to feel uncomfortable, Greg continued.

"Over the past few weeks, I have been meeting with Pastor Bobby and fasting and praying for clarity because I really do not want to hurt anyone again."

Bro, I will be less hurt if you just stop talking. I get it! I am your friend, best friend, amiga, sister in Christ. Fine! I tried to keep my composure as these thoughts went through my mind. I will sit here and nod until he is done. Then we'd get to what we actually came to meet about. Gee wiz. At least God was bringing me clarity. If nothing else, this was answered prayer.

Greg still wasn't done.

"I met with Pastor Bobby because I am in love with you, and

God confirmed that you are to be my wife. Not just my girlfriend, but my wife, and I want to begin courting you."

I was flabbergasted. I never in life had experienced true shock until this moment. I do not know what my face did at this point. I could not move, or think, or speak. The one thought that came to mind was, *Who on earth says "courting" anymore?*

"Should I leave and come back and start again? Do you want to say something?" Greg looked a little deflated. I tried to process what I heard and make sure I really heard what I heard. I looked at Pastor Bobby. He was laughing like someone who had been in on a surprise and is loving the reaction. All of the years of guarding my heart and not giving in, of hoping and trusting, of waiting, it all changed in one moment. Did I even know how to find the words? I had truly never even imagined this scenario, so there was no script to recall. There was just Greg, sitting there in Starbucks, looking at me nervously and probably hoping that he didn't just make a super big fool out of himself.

"I...I love you too," I said, still afraid of the words as they left my mouth. Greg heaved a big sigh of relief. Pastor Bobby gave a joyful laugh. People at tables around us smirked and tried not to look like they were listening in.

Before I could continue processing what on earth just happened, Pastor Bobby got down to business, and it wasn't what I thought. It was the business of Greg and me. I mean, technically it was about the men's and women's ministry because we led those ministries, but it was more. Pastor communicated that we now had to do things like we had never done them before in any relationship. Greg and I had been intimate before, but this time, we would wait until our wedding day (our wedding day, how CRAZY does that sound? Like it's a real thing that would be happening!) We could not leave any doors open, so to speak, so we agreed on some healthy boundaries:

1. Draw closer to God more than ever before.
2. No hanging out at either of our places alone after dark.
3. Wait until after the women's retreat to begin telling people.

We all agreed and prayed. Then we left. I walked into that Starbucks a mighty warrior of singleness—God's daughter who was waiting to see His goodness in the land of the living. In the span of about an hour, everything had changed. Greg took my hand in his as we walked to the car. I felt crazy and elated. It was all still so unreal.

"Hon, do you want to ride with me to drop Pastor Bobby off?" he asked, and it took me a second to realize he was talking to me. He seemed to have no problems with this transition at all.

"Umm, okay," I said.

When we pulled up in front of my house, Greg turned to me and said, "I want to wait until we are engaged to kiss you. I just want to stay focused, okay?"

Again, I agreed, partly suspecting I would wake up from this dream at any point now.

"I'll let you know when I reach home," he said as he kissed me on my forehead. He watched me as I entered my building to make sure I was okay and then he drove away. Kiera had gone upstairs to our place when Charity got home, so I went straight home and to my room. I could not let on to what just happened, and at this point, I could not trust my emotions to stay at bay.

I had no one to talk to but God, and I was so good with sharing this moment with Him. He did just what He said. He ensured that I was pursued, even though I did not even realize that was what was happening. There was no confusion. Greg said he wanted to court me and move toward marriage. There is nothing ambiguous about that. Moreover, he used the word "courting". Who even says courting in New York City? More than I could have imagined, that's what God did. I thanked my Father in Heaven as I lay there in awe, still reeling from the shock of it all. I was headed into a new season. One I never anticipated would ever come, and yet I sensed it coming all at once.

I guess this is the part where I could say thank you for reading and end the book right here, but this is not the end. When our prayer is answered, when we receive that blessing that we have longed for, how we handle those blessings may be one the toughest tests we encounter. Will we stay obedient now that what we have is in our hands? Will we continue to seek God's presence, or will we get consumed by the blessing? This next season is where some deep testing and work begins, and it began with intentionally trying to stay obedient to the boundaries that we had set.

The next morning, it took me a minute to realize I had not

been dreaming and that Greg had indeed professed his love for me the night before. I wanted to call my mom, my accountability partners, and even run to the other room and tell Charity this unbelievable news. However, we had agreed to wait until after the women's retreat, which would be taking place the following weekend. The reason for this was to keep the focus on God and what He was going to do in us during this retreat, and not on how the stalwart example of singleness had nabbed a man after all these years. Of course, my news was definitely a testimony and encouragement that should be shared, but we also did not want the retreat turning into a "I got a man, and you can too" kind of affair. God had to be worthy of praise regardless of my relationship status. I would just have to hold it all a few days more, which was so okay with me because it was still hard for me to even believe.

Later that morning, Greg picked up Kiera and me and we went to the movies. This would not have been a big deal to her as she often hung with me and my friends, including Greg. In my mind though, I thought back to our talk at Orchard Beach, and how she would react when I shared this news with her. It was a date that no one knew about but Greg and me. We were in Jamba Juice and he secretly touched my hand and squeezed it. I wanted to vomit, faint, worship God, and cry all at once. That evening, just as we had discussed, he dropped us off and went on his way to Brooklyn, leaving me with a kiss on my forehead.

Now, you may be thinking, Ummm, weren't you both GROWN adults in your 30s? Why would you be subscribing to what looks like archaic rules and boundaries? If you look at the agreement we decided on as just stringent rules, then it can look and feel like arbitrary rules and unnecessary control. Not hanging out at my place at night? Not even kissing? It wasn't that God had told us explicitly that this is what we were to do. It was that we wanted, above all else, to honor God with our relationship. We knew ourselves and we knew that even though we had years of refining and maturity in our faith, we were still human beings with flesh. The flesh will always function as it is intended to. It will feel and push hard to satisfy its cravings and obey feelings, regardless of consequences. The flesh does not care about what God wants or what is best for us and guess what? The flesh is not going anywhere until we leave our bodies in death. So, the flesh cannot be trusted, not even by the holiest of holy people. That is why we have our spirit. Our spirit is what takes God's guidance into account and it is the spirit that keeps the flesh at bay. In order for our spirit to be in fighting shape, we need to feed it. That is achieved by time in the Word and in prayer. Although the flesh can be a bully, we can weaken its strength by letting it starve as needed. Regular fasting, avoiding distractions and setting boundaries are all necessary at times.

Now that we were in a relationship, it would be easier for us to fall. It's easy to think that eventually you are going to marry this person, so no harm in getting things going a bit early. At night, we are tired, our defenses go down and with no one around, it's easy for one thing to lead to another, especially if you figure this is going to be your life partner. But one thing that Greg told me was that he wanted to present me faultless before God on our wedding day, just as Jesus will do with His bride, the church. Even though I clearly was not physically faultless, I was made a new creature in Christ. I was made clean through grace and that grace gave me every right to conduct myself as if I had never once been with a man. I could start anew with no shame or condemnation. How awesome is our Redeemer? How beautiful was it that I could start all over again and make choices that honored God and kept Him at the center?

When we finally told our mothers, they both told us that they already knew that something was going on between us, even though I had no idea! You know, the mother's intuition thing. Kiera was happy but also a little shocked, like I was. We both knew this would be a completely new season for us and we were excited, but also had no idea what to expect for our little family. My prayer partners and friends were ecstatic to the point of tears for me. As for those who had watched me wait on God against their better judgment, they also got to see firsthand how God can suddenly turn a situation around. Who else but God could get the glory out of how this all happened? That is my favorite part about all of this, that I could say to people that I waited on God and He came through in a way that was undeniably Him. The two major things to come out of all of this —His glory and my growth.

We chose to honor the fact it was no one but God who brought us together, and we created some very tangible steps that helped us to maintain obedience. Greg lived in Brooklyn during this time, and the Brooklyn Bridge was under construction so that meant that the bridge would close at a certain time every night. If we happened to be on a date and were out after the bridge had closed, Greg would go and stay over at my parent's house. Did I mention that my parents have a cat? Did I also mention that Greg is very allergic to cats? This man suffered through allergies so that we could keep ourselves pure. It was that important.

For his birthday late that summer, I made reservations at a Brazilian Churrascaria since he is a meat lover. As a surprise, I also ordered a red velvet cake from his favorite bakery in Brooklyn. Greg had invited his best friend and his wife to join us. This is the same couple whose wedding Greg left Haiti to attend, but I would be meeting them for the first time, and I was nervous. Don and Dorcey were already at the restaurant when we arrived. A few minutes after we all sat down at the table and started chatting, I heard singing behind me:

"Love, a word that comes and goes, but few people really know, what it means to really love somebody…"

I was very familiar with this song as I had sung it with the Ensemble many times. As a matter of fact, I thought, that sounded like the Ensemble. I quickly turned around and saw my fellow Ensemble members standing there in the restaurant, singing. Had I asked them to come and sing? No, I only ordered a cake. I turned back around, puzzled and trying to understand what was happening when I saw Greg begin to get down on one knee in front of me. His lips were moving and he was talking to me, but between the other restaurant patrons noticing what was going on and commenting and sheer shock creating a buzzing in my own ears, I could not hear what he was saying! In my mind, all I could do was still try to put together what was happening. Oh, okay, the Ensemble must have come at Greg's request. He is on one knee, okay, he must be proposing to me. Okay, this is happening. Okay, the people around us see this happening too. They are looking and commenting. To this day, I have no idea what that man was saying, but I do know that he produced a small box with a ring, and I did finally hear him ask me to marry him. Cheers erupted from all around us as he held the ring out. He meant to place it on my finger but I was so in a tizzy that I grabbed it and placed it on my own finger.

Again, without warning, I was absolutely flabbergasted by Greg. I knew that at some point, he intended to propose, but I had no idea he would do it on his own birthday. We had begun dating again about two months prior to this, and now we were going to set a date to be married. I cannot properly communicate to you how surreal this all was for me. I had gone from no prospect in sight to being wooed by an amazing man of God whom I had loved so dearly for so long. Guys, I waited on God's best, and that is exactly what I got.

That night, Greg pulled up to my building and we stepped out of the car. Finally, we would kiss after weeks and weeks of forehead kisses. Just as I began to close my eyes and lean in, Greg said that he now wanted to wait until our wedding day. Now I was a little annoyed—I mean, we had boundaries and accountability, and we were just talking about a kiss for goodness's sake. However, I realized that he was fighting with everything in himself to stay the course and be obedient to God. If that meant we waited to kiss until we were pronounced husband and wife, then so be it. Honestly, what were a few more months compared to the years I had already waited?

Many of you reading this are probably looking at me so side-eyed and thinking we were doing way too much, and maybe for you, it is way too much. That's okay. I am not prescribing my exact journey and the path we chose to walk. I want you to walk your own journey with God at the head of your life, in your own way. What I do want you to consider is that:

> You are God's. Let Him bless your covenant and give you away to your spouse.

God intended sex to take place under the covenant of marriage. There is no gray area when it comes to being in relationship with the love of your life or being engaged. There is nothing that bends the Word of God for you to "get it on" prematurely. You are God's. Let Him bless your covenant and give you away to your spouse.

> Flee from sexual immorality. All other sins a person commits are outside the body, but whoever sins sexually, sins against their own body. Do you not know that your bodies are temples of the Holy Spirit, who is in you, whom you have received from God? You are not your own; you were bought at a price. Therefore honor God with your bodies. (1 Corinthians 6:18–20 NIV)

Just because we are to wait for marriage does not mean that we are not super attracted to our significant other or that we do not get aroused. Like I said before, the flesh does not care about your marital status or your intentions of obeying God. It wants what it craves and it wants it NOW! Don't misinterpret a strong desire with it being right.

> *"Promise me, O women of Jerusalem, not to awaken love until the time is right." (Songs of Solomon 8:4 NIV)*

The same spiritual muscle of restraint that you build up during courtship is the same muscle you will need after marriage. Please believe that there may be times when temptation from outside your covenant will present itself, and you can dig and flex those same muscles of not bending to what you feel, to honor the sanctity of your marriage.

> *"But the fruit of the Spirit is love, joy, peace, forbearance, kindness, goodness, faithfulness, gentleness and self-control." (Galatians 5:22–23 NIV)*

Do what works for your courtship, but be intentional and biblical about it. Decide from the onset what boundaries you can put in place for your relationship instead of just playing it by ear and having to pull back later. If you are already in a relationship, it's not too late to sit down with one another and get in agreement about how you intend to move forward. Seek God for wisdom in your courtship boundaries, and then stay focused on that and not the practical and worldly advice that will inevitably come from many sources. Get some accountability partners that will tell you like it is in love and pray with you through the challenging stuff. Be honest with them. There is such a sweetness to honoring God and inviting Him into your relationship through obedience. It will be challenging at times, but it is so worth it to stay the course.

FOOD *for* THOUGHT

- Do you have accountability partners in place that you can be completely honest with? Do you provide accountability for others? List those people here and utilize them. If you do not currently have anyone in that role, pray about people in your life whom you could ask.

- What are some areas where you think you would need to create boundaries in a premarital relationship?

CHAPTER *Eleven*

PAZIT

arch 26, 2011. My wedding day. I had been up late the night before, well after my bridesmaids had gone to bed. I couldn't sleep. I remember journaling. I was still marveling at God but also lamenting a little for the season of life that would be going away. I truly mourned my singleness. As much as I wanted to be married, I had finally found such peace in my singleness. Life was going to change, and I had no idea just how much. I asked God to keep me, to direct my path and to stay just as dear to me as He always had. I thanked God for making it so clear that I was marrying the right man for me and for Kiera. I asked him to help me to be the best wife and mother that I could be. I cried bittersweet, but mostly sweet tears. I finally made myself lie down and once again pictured myself lying at Jesus' feet, the shadow of His wings covering me and protecting me. I felt immensely loved and drifted to sleep.

As the bridal party and I walked out of the hotel lobby, I felt all eyes on us. It seemed insane that this time, I was the bride. But I was. This was my day and I was wearing my Pronovias dress just as I had seen in Spain. That morning was crisp and clear. The skies were a brilliant blue, but it was also windy and still quite nippy. However,

I could not even feel the cold as I walked out of the limo and into the vestibule of the church. I was already crying, and they were ugly tears—happy tears but not cute at all. I remember warning Selina to try and cry pretty on her wedding day for photo's sake, and here I was, ignoring my own advice and putting the makeup artist's skills to the ultimate test. Finally, one of my friends sternly told me to get it together and smile right before the doors opened and the music started playing. I dabbed my handkerchief under my eyes and took a deep breath. This was it. I was walking down the aisle.

I have been to many weddings where people don't exactly show up for the ceremony, just the reception. Our ceremony started at 10am on a Saturday. That's early for many people. Yet as I walked down the aisle, I saw face after beaming face of friends and family who had come to witness what God had done. I even had a friend who was nine months pregnant waddle her way to the church that morning just to witness this momentous day. Our ceremony was far from the dry and short versions that we see on TV and in movies. It was a full-out worship service! I could no longer hold in my emotion and there are pictures of both Greg and me at the altar, our hands lifted in worship and crying some ugly and happy tears before God.

The songs had been meticulously chosen as ones that were close to us, and of course, the Ensemble was there in full force to sing us into praise and worship. Greg and the groomsmen walked out to "Moving Forward", a song about leaving the past behind and God making all things new. I walked out to "Agnus Dei", which was simply a worship song unto the Lord, declaring His power and holiness. We wanted every person in attendance to know that all glory was for God. He had done this. Beatrice, the same one who pondered with me on the phone all of those years back, sang a beautiful solo. Minister Cheryl, who had been a mentor to the both of us, prayed over our union. Pastor Bobby, who sat patiently and let me cry in his office and asked me to pray for Greg and do nothing more than that—presided over our ceremony. After we exchanged rings, we had Kiera come up and Greg read to her from an inscription he had engraved onto a locket. He placed the locket around her neck. He would now be her father. We were a family. People sobbed audibly. All of our fellow leaders were invited to come up and pray with us. Pastor Bobby's father, Bishop Lewis, came up from Virginia Beach and the final moments of our ceremony were spoken by him. Finally, the moment arrived for us to be pronounced husband and wife. Finally, the words were uttered that I had waited for. "You may kiss the bride". I am told that I displayed the same proactive enthusiasm as the night that Greg proposed and pulled his face close to mine and planted one right on him. I kissed him. I kissed my husband.

At our reception, each table centerpiece was a paper lantern with Isaiah 43:19 printed:

Behold, I am doing a new thing! Now it springs up;
Do you not perceive it?

Nothing could have been more accurate about what God had

done in my life. This was the beginning of a new thing, a new season, a promise fulfilled. God's Word had not returned void. It had been a long road, exhausting at times, exhilarating at others, but God was there every step of the way and I discovered that He was the most important part of it all. I didn't want any of it if it wasn't with Him.

My courtship and wedding day were just like a fairy tale. I absolutely could not have asked for anything more. I had indeed been tried in the fire and I had come forth as pure gold. I am so glad it all happened the way it did. I am glad I was a hot sizzling mess. I am so glad I ran from God and made mistakes and was not some poster child for perfect Christianity. I was a statistic; a young single mom only technically not considered a teen mom by a few months. I am glad for it. I am glad I was broken. I am glad I had to have my life turned upside down. I am glad I got my heart broken. I am glad that Jesus was the only one who could mend it. I am glad I was lonely and isolated. I am glad that in that isolation, I found a relationship with God. I am glad I had to wait. I am glad that in the waiting, God grew me up and showed me real love. I am glad that God surprised me with a sweet and beautiful love with Greg. I am glad that no one else can take credit for it but God.

I am glad to be able to share this all with you. My lowest and highest moments are all poured out for you because I am no different than you. Now you know, you know that even someone as wrecked as me is still loved deeply by God. God loves you like that too. Wherever you are right now in life, it matters not. God loves you so much and has redemptive and surprising plans for you. It is not too late for you. You are not defined by your sin and you should not be ashamed. You are washed by the blood of sweet, powerful Jesus and you are not under condemnation. You are God's precious daughter and He has more for you than what you see right now.

This is not even about finding a man and getting married. That just happens to be one of the stories God chose to use as an example of his power and overwhelming grace in my life. If this book is about finding a husband, then it's all wrong. This is about believing that no matter what you have done, no matter what has been done to you and no matter where you are today, God has a plan for you. A good plan that He alone would be able to get the credit for. So, it may be very hard at times. You may cry on a bathroom floor. You may have to let go of some things you have gotten used to. You may have to allow change to occur in your life. You may have people wanting to fix it for you. You may have to watch others get blessed and you will certainly need to be a blessing.

> *You will be strengthened and beautified, and you too will come forth as pure gold. Start calling yourself Pazit now.*

Stay the course and stay in His presence. Seek God and allow Him to show you the things that need to go, whether forever or for a season. That part is none of your business. Make your business loving and learning God. Fall in love with Jesus. Let love overtake you and share it with others. Stay in that refiner's fire. I know it gets so hot and uncomfortable in there. I know it all too well. But you

will not burn up. You will not be consumed. You will be strengthened and beautified, and you too will come forth as pure gold. Start
calling yourself *Pazit* now.

NOTES

CHAPTER *Six*

1. Gold, M. (2020) Stages of Change. *Psych Central*. Retrieved on September 6, 2020, from https://psychcentral.com/lib/stages-of-change/

2. Dictionary.com, s.v. "ambivalence," accessed August 10, 2020 https://www.dictionary.com/browse/ambivalence

3. Dictionary.com, s.v. "diet," accessed August 10, 2020 https://www.dictionary.com/browse/diet

CPSIA information can be obtained
at www.ICGtesting.com
Printed in the USA
FSHW012230291120
76319FS